PEACE IS A CHAIN REACTION

How World War II Japanese Balloon Bombs
Brought People of Two Nations Together

TANYA LEE STONE

CANDLEWICK PRESS

Foreword by Ben Takeshita

Illustrations by Yumeno Furukawa

Archival images curated by Tanya Lee Stone

*The endpapers illustrate all the known balloon bomb sighting,
landing, or recovery locations in the United States and Mexico.*

• • •

First edition 2022

Library of Congress Catalog Card Number 2022901780
ISBN 978-0-7636-7686-5

22 23 24 25 26 27 LEO 10 9 8 7 6 5 4 3 2 1

Printed in Heshan, Guangdong, China

This book was typeset in Plantin.
The illustrations are etchings, edited digitally.

Candlewick Press
99 Dover Street
Somerville, Massachusetts 02144

www.candlewick.com

A JUNIOR LIBRARY GUILD SELECTION

For Yuzuru John Takeshita, for the victims of every kind of war and every act of hate, and for the people who fight for justice. Many overlap.

•   •   •

Ben and Yuzuru Takeshita

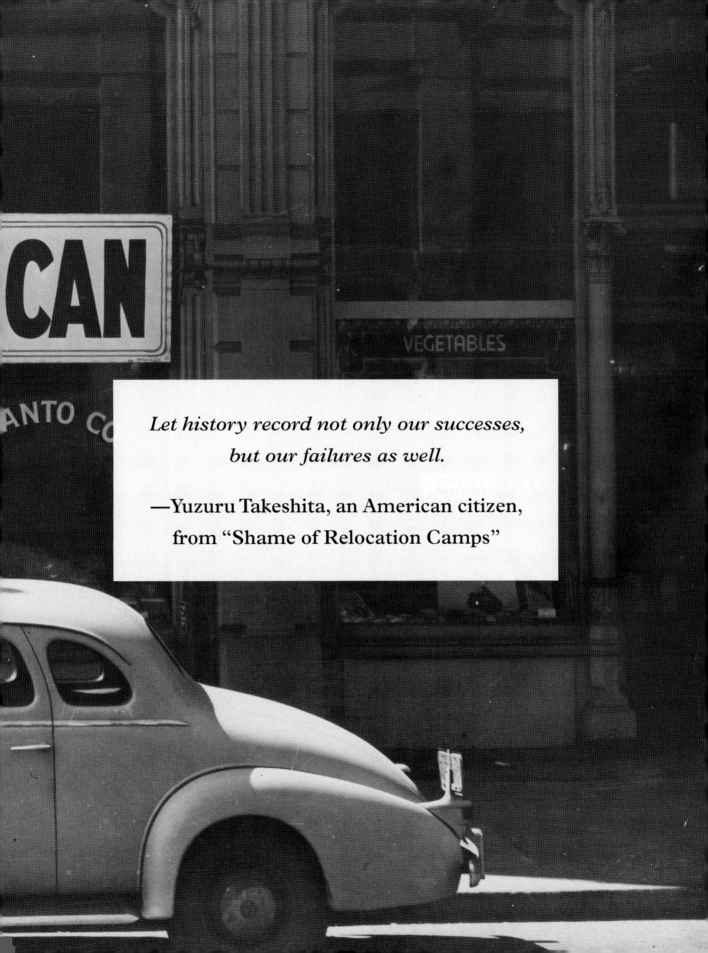

*Let history record not only our successes,
but our failures as well.*

—Yuzuru Takeshita, an American citizen,
from "Shame of Relocation Camps"

CONTENTS

FOREWORD

Since the story of my older brother Yuzuru John Takeshita is a main focus of *Peace Is a Chain Reaction*, Tanya Lee Stone kindly sent me the manuscript to read prior to publication. We had corresponded several times before, and she was familiar with the oral history interviews I'd done through the organization Densho about my family's World War II experience and my own postwar experiences. My conversations with Tanya provided her with additional family context for the larger story that my older brother sparked through his interactions with the groups of people you will read about here.

From the moment I started reading the prologue of this book, I couldn't stop until I had read the entire manuscript to see how all the varied pieces of this narrative would unfold. I was only eleven years old when World War II started for us here in America, on December 7, 1941, and my parents hid their worries from us younger children. As an adult, though, I have been quite active in thinking and talking about all that happened, since being aware of the past can help us prevent future mistakes. Yet even quite recently, politicians have referenced what happened to Japanese Americans as a precedent to justify the imprisonment of undocumented immigrants, and so it is clear that keeping history alive is crucial.

I was very curious as to how Tanya Lee Stone was going to tell my brother's interesting and complicated story for young readers. I was surprised and impressed with her detailed writing, weaving quotes from people into the telling of this history. From the beginning of her book, it will be obvious to you how much research she has done to get this story told. From describing how World War II affected people throughout the world to showing how a small group of young girls in Japan was affected to telling how John brought two groups from each side of the conflict together in the small town of Bly, Oregon, it is amazing to me that Tanya was able to narrate these various threads so delicately and with such sensitivity for the feelings of all the people involved.

This story is a beautiful example of how innocent people from two different nations were able to show respect for each other and resolve things peacefully even though they had once been at war. Inspired by my older brother, all of these individuals chose to take action, to forgive, and to show peace toward one another.

Without any further writing, I shall leave it up to all of you interested readers to learn how one seemingly small piece of history deeply affected people in both Japan and the United States. We should all strive to respect each other's differences, understand each other, and live peaceful lives together. This story is proof that it can be done.

I want to thank Tanya Lee Stone for preserving this important history.

—*Ben Takeshita*

PROLOGUE

From a very young age, we can be taught to hate or fear people who are different from us. Sometimes this racism is buried so deep, it can be hard to see. Sometimes it is clearly visible. War is one of the more obvious ways in which entire nations can be taught to hate—and fear—people of other nations.

What you are about to read is just one small story of how one small group of people eventually realized their part in an enormous story of fear and hate called World War II. This war took the lives of hundreds of millions of people. Casualty numbers like "hundreds of millions" are difficult to wrap our minds around. It can feel abstract, less real, less personal. But six? Six specific lives lost are easy to imagine.

Some of the people you will meet in this true story are a group of Japanese women who discovered, decades after World War II ended, how deeply responsible they felt for six lost American lives. Their feelings compelled them to make amends. They didn't have to do this. No one was holding them responsible. In fact, these women were children at the time of those American deaths and were only following their nation's orders. Still, they felt remorse.

This remorse is a testimony to the ties that connect us all as human beings. No matter our perceived differences, we are all citizens sharing the same home planet. We all have common needs—a safe place to live, enough food to eat, clean air to breathe, clean water to drink. And the freedom to live our lives in peace.

Fear and hatred, war—they rip those dreams of peace to shreds. Adults wage war, while children are unwitting victims, pulled in without any choice—and often with little or no knowledge.

This is a story about two groups of children on opposite sides of the world, forever connected by an act of war.

This is a story about the adults some of those children became, forever connected by acts of forgiveness, understanding, and peace.

And this is a story about one remarkable man whose heart belonged to both nations and who set that peace and understanding in motion for everyone involved.

CHAPTER ONE

School would be out soon. All the fun that summer promised was almost close enough to touch for thirteen-year-old Diane Shoemaker. But on a bright spring day in May 1945, in one swift instant, her world turned dark and dire. Soon instead of dreaming up ways to pass the lazy days ahead, Diane was seething with rage. It was impossible for her to imagine how she would ever feel okay again.

Her brother was gone, his life taken suddenly and violently, and she was gripped by a blinding desire to avenge his senseless death and set the world right again.

She was not alone in this response to her grief. Diane's cousin shared her anger. Together, the two teens contemplated carrying out a plot to blow up the Tule Lake Relocation Center, in California. Tule Lake, just across the state line, was about an hour's drive south from their home in Bly, Oregon. At its peak, there were nearly nineteen thousand people of Japanese descent being held there by the American government. The United States, at war with Japan, had decided that people of Japanese descent posed a threat, even though many of them were American citizens. But Diane and her cousin weren't aware of any of that. They were only imagining the faces of the people they had been taught to think of as the enemy. Tule Lake became the target of their fury.

What terrible tragedy could have caused two young people to feel such despair, such desperation, that they might even consider committing such a heinous crime?

CHAPTER TWO

To tell this story, we have to go back about three and a half years, to December 7, 1941. President Franklin Delano Roosevelt called this "a date which will live in infamy." And indeed, it affected countless millions of people—from the laser focus of Diane Shoemaker and the people in her small corner of the world, to a broad camera angle that encircled the globe. Like the first domino to fall in an infinite chain, what happened on December 7, 1941, triggered events in America that had a ripple effect—not only on the course of World War II but also on entire nations and, in fact, on the very state of our world ever since. How? Out of the devastation and destruction of World War II came our international peacekeeping organization, the United Nations (which created the Universal Declaration of Human Rights), and the roots of the World Trade Organization, established to help avoid worldwide economic depression—another casualty of war. But we're getting ahead of ourselves. Here's how it went down.

(Above) Former First Lady Eleanor Roosevelt holding a large display copy of the Universal Declaration of Human Rights. This document was created three years after World War II ended and serves as a global milestone of human rights.

HOW AMERICA GOT INVOLVED IN WORLD WAR II

In the Pacific region of the world, the spark of World War II was ignited when Japan invaded China in 1931 and started setting up a Japanese state in that nation. By 1938, Japan occupied much of China. In 1940, Japanese troops invaded French Indochina and entered into the Axis alliance with Germany and Italy.

Meanwhile, in Europe, trouble began brewing in 1939. In late August of that year, Germany (under the dictatorship of Adolf Hitler) and the Soviet Union (under the dictatorship of Joseph Stalin) made a pact not

Political cartoonist Clifford Berryman created a recurring character named Miss Democracy to personify America. In this July 1941 piece, Berryman is showing America's perceived disinterest in joining the war, despite the Soviet Union's call for assistance.

to engage in war with each other—right before they waged war on their neighbors. Germany invaded Poland on September 1, 1939, and two days later, in response, Great Britain and France declared war on Germany. Right on Germany's heels, the Soviet Union invaded Finland, occupied part of Poland, and took over Latvia, Estonia, and Lithuania.

The war quickly escalated, with Germany invading Norway, the Netherlands, Denmark, Belgium, Luxembourg, and France. Then Italy (under the dictatorship of Benito Mussolini) declared war on Great Britain and France.

Where did the United States fit into this mess? The majority of the American people wanted to stay out of the war; the overall feeling was one of isolationism. The nation was weary, having suffered through World War I and the Great Depression. Americans did not want to participate in the war through military action. After Japan occupied the French colony of Indochina, though, the US government took action by stopping steel, iron, and aviation fuel from being sent to Japan, but they only limited (rather than banning) the export of oil. The United States also offered to help Great Britain and France, sending supplies to both of those nations. But when the Germans began to use submarines to sink American ships carrying those supplies, the situation intensified.

In September 1940, Germany, Italy, and Japan signed a treaty to join forces against Great Britain and France. This treaty served as a warning to the United States to stop helping those two nations. And by March 1941, although America was still not at war, it had increased its aid to England.

Three months later, Germany broke its nonaggression pact with the Soviet Union, invading that nation. And although the Germans had sunk unarmed American supply ships already, in October 1941 the situation grew even more volatile when a German submarine torpedoed a US Navy warship—sinking it and killing 115 crew members. Then Japan, with its military-led government, got a new prime minister: former war minister General Hideki Tojo. The following month, the United States called on Japan to withdraw from China and Indochina and stopped all American oil sales to Japan. The friction between Japan and the United States had roots that stretched back decades and had to do with competing for resources in China and other parts of Asia. The two countries had managed to navigate a careful dance around these competing interests for a long time, but now the tension between Japan and the United States was increasing by the minute. The situation was literally about to explode.

"THE SKY WAS JUST BLACK WITH SMOKE"

Ted Tsukiyama was born and raised in Honolulu, Hawaii. In December 1941, he was a student at the University of Hawaii and a member of the Reserve Officers' Training Corps (ROTC).

Pearl Harbor, near Honolulu, is home to a US naval base where warships and military personnel were in position, readying for war, if or when it became necessary to mobilize. The Japanese knew that if they destroyed the US fleet sitting in Pearl Harbor, it would severely limit America's ability

Shown here in uniform, Ted Tsukiyama served as a member of the Hawaii Territorial Guard, which was formed shortly after the Pearl Harbor attack. This photo was likely taken between December 1941 and January 1942, because the Guard's Japanese American members were removed on January 19, 1942.

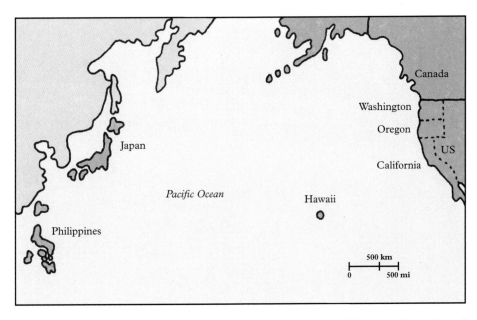

This map shows the relative distances between Japan, the Philippines, Hawaii, and the western coast of the United States.

to engage in the war in the Pacific. But the United States, even though it was fairly certain Japan was planning an attack of *some* kind, firmly believed that Japan would most likely strike the Philippines (then a commonwealth of the United States), as it was much closer (half the distance) to Japan than Hawaii was.

That was why, at a little before 8:00 a.m. on December 7, 1941, Pearl Harbor was thrown into a frenzied chaos when nearly two hundred Japanese fighter planes began roaring overhead, one wave after another, in a full-blown surprise attack. Sailors and soldiers scrambled to defend the base. Tsukiyama's group was the first ROTC unit called to respond. "The sky was just black with smoke . . . and just rumbling thunder," he recalled. "They issued us bullets and put firing pins in the rifles and we were ready; we were at war."

A small boat rescues a USS West Virginia crew member from the water as the battleship burns. The ship was hit by at least two bombs and seven torpedoes during the Pearl Harbor attack.

But the damage Japan inflicted was swift and devastating. Within two hours, the Japanese pilots had destroyed 188 US aircraft, sunk four out of eight American battleships positioned in Pearl Harbor, and disabled the rest. More than 2,400 Americans were killed.

Japan, however, had miscalculated. Instead of keeping the United States *out* of the war, its attack on Pearl Harbor had the exact opposite effect. It was the tipping point. America could no longer avoid entering World War II. The next day, President Roosevelt—in an address later known as his "Day of Infamy" speech, which was broadcast on the radio to the American public—called upon Congress to declare that since "the unprovoked and dastardly attack by Japan on Sunday, December 7, 1941, a state of war has existed between the United States and the Japanese Empire." The anger in the president's voice could be heard loud and clear.

Roosevelt urged Americans to "remember the character of the onslaught against us." His address was met with thunderous applause, as the assembled Congress rose to its feet. This was the first formal action the United States took against the Japanese. The cause and effect seemed straightforward.

But another action was about to be carried out by the United States, and this time it was on its own soil and against its own citizens—those of Japanese descent. There was *nothing* straightforward about it.

"WE HAD THE FACE OF THE ENEMY"

The animosity and suspicion toward people who looked Japanese was immediate. Without any regard toward rights of citizenship, they became targets. One American serviceman recalled the treatment he got while responding to the Pearl Harbor attack. "The radio said, 'This is the real thing; report to Post,'" recounted Jesse Hirata, a later member of the 100th Infantry Battalion, which was made up mostly of Japanese Americans from Hawaii. "So, we jumped in my cousin's car, three of us, and we got stuck right in front of Pearl Harbor . . . the bombers were still coming. . . . I jumped out to look at all the smoke and the bombs going off." His comment was punctuated with nervous laughter. "Then the SP [Shore Patrol] comes to me with a pistol and sticks it in my side, and says 'This is a Jap.'" Ted Tsukiyama remembered feeling uneasy that day as well. "There was suddenly the concern, that hey, y'know, the enemy is the same race as we are."

Within hours of the attack, the US Federal Bureau of Investigation (FBI) went on the hunt for any Japanese people they thought could be spies or otherwise helping the Japanese government. The FBI started rounding up and arresting Japanese leaders of communities—heads of Japanese associations, priests, and even Japanese language teachers. Government officials closed down Japanese banks, stores, and newspapers, locking owners out of their own businesses. In the homes of Japanese people who were not American citizens but were parents or grandparents of American-born Japanese, officials rushed in and ransacked their personal belongings, looking for any evidence that they might be loyal to the emperor of Japan. Some white Americans began panicking as well, especially those living along the West Coast, where the majority of Japanese people living in the continental United States resided. They started lashing out against their fellow Americans.

The racism was rampant.

The situation was so egregious that the *Los Angeles Times* called California "a zone of danger." Overnight, friends became enemies. Anyone who looked Japanese was regarded with suspicion. The newsreels that typically ran in movie theaters before a featured film were filled with propaganda about Japanese people. "They put such fear into people that we were the enemy," California high school student Alice Imamoto Takemoto said. "The hostility was all around." Sumi Seki, the wife of a Japanese American military man, described it vividly: "We had the face of the enemy." People of Japanese descent were living in fear of being deemed a threat to their own nation.

Jiro Ishihara, a Japanese American high school student in Los Angeles, recalled, "We'd hear that the person down the street had been picked up for having feudal dolls [an innocent Japanese toy] and that a neighbor had been taken away for having Japanese recordings. So my father burned everything that had the slightest connection to Japan. . . . It was a terrible time."

First Lady Eleanor Roosevelt knew how wrong and devastating this approach was. On December 16, 1941, in her newspaper column "My Day"—which she wrote six days a week—she counseled Americans that "the great mass of our people, stemming from these various national ties, must not feel they have suddenly ceased to be Americans." But her warning fell on deaf ears. In fact, she was criticized for it. The *Los Angeles Times* published one editorial that read: "When she starts bemoaning the plight of the treacherous snakes we call Japanese, with apologies to all snakes, she has reached the point where she should be forced to retire from public life."

Incredibly, a story in the December 22, 1941, issue of *Life* magazine actually went so far as to point out physical differences between Chinese and Japanese people, so that racist behavior toward Japanese people wouldn't mistakenly be directed at Chinese people. The piece was horribly bigoted. It instructed readers that a Chinese person "is relatively tall and slenderly built. His complexion is parchment yellow, his face long and

Despite the fact that Germany and Italy were allies with Japan, Germans and Italians in America did not suffer anywhere near the level of racism inflicted on Japanese people in America.

14

delicately boned," while a Japanese person "betrays aboriginal antecedents in a squat, long-torsoed build, a broader, more massively boned head and face, flat, often pug nose, yellow-ocher skin and heavier beard."

This racial profiling—as we would rightly call it today—infected the West Coast of America like a disease. And as terrible as that was, things were about to get much worse.

"WE KNEW THAT SOME AMONG THEM WERE POTENTIALLY DANGEROUS"

On February 19, 1942, about two months after FDR gave his "Day of Infamy" speech calling for war on Japan, the president issued Executive Order 9066, giving the US government the authority to "prescribe military areas in such places and of such extent" as it may determine, "from which any or all persons may be excluded, and with respect to which, the right of any person to enter, remain in, or leave shall be subject to whatever restrictions the Secretary of War or the appropriate Military Commander may impose."

Always pay attention to language. There is *power* in language. Let's break that quote down. To "prescribe military areas in such places and of such extent" basically means that the government had the power to choose *where* those places would be and to what degree—or *how*—they would be affected. The next part, "from which any or all persons," meant that the government got to say *who* was affected. And "the right of any person to enter, remain in, or leave shall be subject to whatever restrictions . . . the appropriate Military Commander may impose" meant that the military pretty much had free rein to do as it pleased.

By signing this order, FDR handed the US government ultimate power over the choices, the decisions, the fates—the *lives*—of whomever it deemed necessary. But wait. As American citizens, you might be thinking, aren't those people's rights protected by the Constitution? Apparently not.

A Los Angeles storefront, April 1942, just before the owners underwent forced removal

As soon as Executive Order 9066 was signed, the target of "any or all persons" was made crystal clear: people of Japanese descent, whether they had been born in America or not. The rationale was put forth by the government that, after Pearl Harbor, Japan might attack the American West Coast. That logic quickly extended to the notion that any person of Japanese descent might be sympathetic to the enemy, thereby posing a danger to America. Approximately 120,000 people of Japanese descent—the majority of the Japanese-descent population in the continental United States—lived in California, Oregon, and Washington, and a mandatory "relocation" process began, with Lieutenant General John DeWitt determining the "prescribed military areas" previously unspecified in Executive Order 9066. DeWitt was the commanding general of the Western Defense Command, which was charged with defending the western portion of America. His designation of the prescribed military areas? All of California, the western halves of Washington and Oregon, and the southern part of Arizona. No matter that two-thirds of the people

(Right) Taken by Dorothea Lange on April 11, 1942, this close-up image documents the exclusion order posted at First and Front Streets directing the removal of persons of Japanese ancestry from the first area in San Francisco to be affected by the forced incarceration.

16

WESTERN DEFENSE COMMAND AND FOURTH ARMY
WARTIME CIVIL CONTROL ADMINISTRATION
Presidio of San Francisco, California
April 1, 1942

INSTRUCTIONS
TO ALL PERSONS OF
JAPANESE
ANCESTRY

Living in the Following Area:

All that portion of the City and County of San Francisco, State of California, lying generally west of the north-south line established by Junipero Serra Boulevard, Worchester Avenue, and Nineteenth Avenue, and lying generally north of the east-west line established by California Street, to the intersection of Market Street, and thence on Market Street to San Francisco Bay.

All Japanese persons, both alien and non-alien, will be evacuated from the above designated area by 12:00 o'clock noon Tuesday, April 7, 1942.

No Japanese person will be permitted to enter or leave the above described area after 8:00 a. m., Thursday, April 2, 1942, without obtaining special permission from the Provost Marshal at the Civil Control Station located at:

> 1701 Van Ness Avenue
> San Francisco, California

The Civil Control Station is equipped to assist the Japanese population affected by this evacuation in the following ways:

1. Give advice and instructions on the evacuation.

2. Provide services with respect to the management, leasing, sale, storage or other disposition of most kinds of property including: real estate, business and professional equipment, buildings, household goods, boats, automobiles, livestock, etc.

3. Provide temporary residence elsewhere for all Japanese in family groups.

4. Transport persons and a limited amount of clothing and equipment to their new residence, as specified below.

The Following Instructions Must Be Observed:

1. A responsible member of each family, preferably the head of the family, or the person in whose name most of the property is held, and each individual living alone, will report to the Civil Control Station to receive further instructions. This must be done between 8:00 a. m. and 5:00 p. m., Thursday, April 2, 1942, or between 8:00 a. m. and

of Japanese descent living there had been born and raised in America and had no connection to Japan outside of their heritage. DeWitt's designation was made official after little more than ten minutes of discussion in the House and Senate, during which a law was passed that incorporated Executive Order 9066 and made violating it a criminal offense.

What did this mean? It meant that more than 120,000 people of Japanese descent living in America were being involuntarily moved to what were called "relocation," or "internment," centers. There were ten of them.

After the implementation of Executive Order 9066, Milton Eisenhower—head of the War Relocation Authority (WRA), which was created for the purpose of carrying out the order—hosted and narrated a short newsreel designed to explain to the general public just why this executive order was necessary. You might also call this film a piece of wartime propaganda—that is, information presented in a way intended to support a particular political point of view. "When the Japanese attacked Pearl Harbor," Eisenhower said, "our west coast became a potential combat zone. . . . We knew that some among them were potentially dangerous. No one knew what would happen among them if Japanese forces should try to invade our shores. Military authorities therefore determined that all of them, citizens and aliens alike, would have to move."

Eisenhower went on to include such ridiculous reasons for suspicion as: "Japanese fishermen had every opportunity to watch the movement of our ships" and "Japanese farmers were living close to vital aircraft plants."

The terms *internment, relocation,* and *evacuation* are often still used to refer to this historical event, but *internment* means "the legally permissible detention of enemy aliens in time of war" and *evacuation* implies that the action was taken for the safety of the people affected. Throughout this book, unless in quotation marks or as a proper noun, I've chosen to follow the terminology supported by the Densho organization—a nonprofit dedicated to preserving and sharing this history to promote equity and justice—and use the more accurate terms *incarceration* or *detainment* instead of *internment,* and *forced removal* instead of *relocation* or *evacuation.*

Notice the use of the word *our* here, and remember that Eisenhower is referring mostly to American citizens, implying that they are not included in—or are in opposition to—the concept of *our*.

In what might be described as a fatherly tone, he then laid out how well the "migration" was being handled: "Neither the Army nor the War Relocation Authority relished the idea of taking men, women, and children from their homes, their shops, and their farms, so the military and civilian agencies alike determined to do the job as a democracy should, with real consideration for the people involved." He then made note of

On the day after Pearl Harbor, an Oakland, California, store owner (and University of California graduate) posted this sign. Once Executive Order 9066 went into effect, the store was closed and the owner detained. This image is another example of photographer Dorothea Lange's documentation of this time.

how cooperative the detainees were, saying, "The many loyal among them felt that this was a sacrifice they could make in behalf of America's war effort."

Saying "the many loyal among them," however, implied that there were also many *disloyal* among them. In actual fact, during the entire course of the war, there were only ten people in America convicted of spying for Japan. *None* of them were Japanese.

Remember, language is power. It is possible to take something awful, explain it away calmly, and give it a bland label to try to make it more easily digested or ignored by a general audience. It's always important to question the meanings of things for yourself.

The WRA used similar tactics in documenting the forced removal and life in the "camps," as they were called. It made short films showing serene detainees painting, exuberant young men playing baseball, laughing girls walking to their school where teachers taught a curriculum similar to what they would have had at home. The WRA also hired photographers, including famous photographer Dorothea Lange, to create well-curated images of cooperative, smiling people appearing to enjoy—or at least be making the most of—their current situation. Why? So the WRA could present a palatable view of the incarceration of innocent people to the world. Dorothea Lange did *not* capture the positive images the WRA was counting on, so they impounded the bulk of her photographs—including the negatives, prints, and undeveloped film.

The real picture did not emerge for a long time, and it came through the firsthand accounts of people who were incarcerated and later revealed their real experiences—joys as well as sorrows—in interviews, articles, letters, books, and documentaries. (They had not initially been allowed to bring cameras with them.)

After the war, the army quietly deposited Dorothea Lange's work in the National Archives, and now we have free access to them.

Toyo Miyatake was a successful photographer when he, his wife, and their four children were incarcerated at Manzanar, one of the ten detention centers. He managed to smuggle in a camera lens and film plate holder and, through a series of clever moves, ended up photographing daily life at Manzanar. Miyatake took the above photograph of detainees playing baseball.

Famous photographer Ansel Adams also documented life at Manzanar. He focused on close-up portraits he described as intending to show resilience amid hardship (such as "farmer with cabbages" or "girl and volleyball"). Many criticized Adams for avoiding the more realistic content Dorothea Lange chose to show.

Miyatake and Adams met at Manzanar, and their work was later published together in a book titled *Two Views of Manzanar*. The portrait of Miyatake above was taken by Adams.

Photographed by Dorothea Lange on April 7, 1942, a San Francisco store owner boards up his shop before being detained.

More than 120,000 people were "migrated," sent to "relocation" or "internment" centers, and deemed "internees" or "evacuees." This "move" was mandatory. The full force of their own government powered this blatant racism. This number included American-born Japanese serving in the US military. Their service made no difference in how they were treated, and General DeWitt made his thoughts on that matter clear. In the documentary *Beyond Barbed Wire*, about the US Army's 442nd Regimental Combat Team, composed almost entirely of American-born Japanese, historian Shigeya Kihara said, "Regarding Japanese Americans in the military, General DeWitt publicly stated, 'A Jap is a Jap.'" DeWitt is also on record as saying, "There isn't such a thing as a loyal Japanese and it is just impossible to determine their loyalty by investigation—it just can't be done."

"WE WENT WITH JUST ONE SUITCASE"

What did "relocating" 120,000 people entail? People were fired from their jobs, their businesses were shut down and/or confiscated, and they were forced to leave their homes and their livelihoods. "My father had a jewelry store for thirty years and we were doing really well. . . . We lost everything,"

The 442nd Regimental Combat Team, which included the 100th Infantry Battalion and the 442nd Infantry Regiment, remains the most highly decorated unit of its size in US military history.

22

Toy Kanegai remembered. "We just had to leave our cars, our house, furniture, all behind us, and walk out the door. We went with just one suitcase."

To say, as Eisenhower did during his initial WRA newscast, that "the quick disposal of property often involved financial sacrifice for the evacuees" was a gigantic understatement that severely downplayed the reality of what people were subjected to. It was not only most of their personal belongings that had to be left behind, either. Family pets were usually not allowed to go with them. Some managed to find neighbors or friends to care for their beloved pets, and some were eventually reunited. Others were not.

A busload of people about to be transported from their homes in a Japanese neighborhood in San Francisco. This bus is en route to the Tanforan Assembly Center. Within a few days of this image being taken, the onlookers of Japanese descent will also have been detained. Photo by Dorothea Lange.

This forced removal affected entire families. "My brother and I were in the living room looking out the front window," famed actor and activist George Takei remembers, "and we saw two soldiers marching up our driveway. They carried bayonets on their rifles. They stomped up the front porch and banged on the door. My father answered it, and the soldiers ordered us out of our home. . . . I will never be able to forget that scene. It is burned into my memory."

While many families were kept together, some were torn apart—especially when one or both parents were deemed suspicious. In one

San Francisco residents form a line outside the Japanese American Citizens League Auditorium to be "processed" before being incarcerated. Photo by Dorothea Lange, April 1942.

instance, a fifteen-year-old girl arrived home from school to discover her parents had been taken because they were Japanese-language teachers, which meant, in the eyes of the military, they could be guilty of aiding the enemy. The girl and her three older sisters then had to figure out what to do with their house and everything in it before being sent to a temporary "assembly center," where they lived in a horse stall for many months before being moved to a "relocation center," where they were finally reunited with their parents.

One-third of all the Japanese people who were incarcerated were children and teenagers. One-*third*.

One of them was Yuzuru Takeshita (pronounced tah-kesh-tah).

On April 20, 1942, Dorothea Lange took this photograph of children pledging allegiance to the flag at the Raphael Weill Public School in San Francisco. By May 20, all of the city's children and families of Japanese descent had been detained. In this photo, Lange juxtaposes innocent classmates and their act of patriotism with the terrible reality of what happened to them.

CHAPTER THREE

Yuzuru Takeshita was born in California (making him an American citizen) in March 1926. His father, Manzo Takeshita, and mother, Hatsumi Ikeda, were both from the same area in Kyushu, Japan, but had not known each other there. They both happened to move to California when they were teenagers, joining their fathers, who had been working as farmhands. They later met, married, and began a family. Yuzuru was their third son. The Takeshita family grew large—six sons (although, sadly, the second son died in infancy) and three daughters.

Yuzuru was an excellent student—and a busy one! Through third grade, he attended his elementary school, as well as a Japanese-language school and a Buddhist Sunday school.

The summer after third grade, when he was nine years old, his mother accompanied him and his older brother Spencer to Japan (two of their sisters and two of their younger brothers were also along for the ride). Aboard

(Above) Yuzuru Takeshita's parents, Manzo and Hatsumi Takeshita

The Asama Maru

the *Asama Maru*, a massive Japanese ocean liner that held more than eight hundred passengers and had a crew of 330, the Takeshitas set sail from California. Yuzuru made quick friends with one of the crew, who showed him all over the ship, even taking him and another boy to the engine room to explain how the ship was powered. Yuzuru was enthralled. But the ocean crossing was only the beginning.

Yuzuru and Spencer were on their way to live with their maternal grandfather for a few years. Their grandfather, who had lived in the United States for twenty-five years, had returned to Japan the year before his grandsons came to stay. The boys were going to learn Japanese and experience their heritage firsthand. Also, as Ben Takeshita, one of Yuzuru's younger brothers, later explained, sending American-born Japanese children to spend time with their relatives in Japan was "customary in those days because of racial job discrimination in the United States . . . so that when they became adults, they could maybe get a better paying job with a Japanese company, which were moving to the United States to set up their businesses in the 1920s through 1941."

Two years earlier, the *Asama Maru* had carried the Japanese Olympic team to Los Angeles for the 1932 Olympics.

"I HAD FORGOTTEN ENGLISH ALTOGETHER"

It took Yuzuru a little while to adjust to school in Japan. Back in California, he had been a top student, but his Japanese-language skills, despite the extra lessons, were not on par with those of his Japanese classmates. He struggled, and his self-esteem suffered. "I began to detest school, frequently feigning illness and begging to stay at home," he later wrote. After his mother and the school principal figured out that he should go down one level for a while so that he could get up to speed, the situation greatly improved. Once she felt her two sons were both adjusting to life in Japan, their mother returned home to California with their other siblings.

A hardworking student and a fast learner, Yuzuru had earned top honors by the end of fifth grade. He was a fast runner, too, often winning first place in field-day races. He was happy in Japan (although some unease was now part of the backdrop, as war had broken out with China a year earlier, in July 1936). By the time Yuzuru was in sixth grade, he had joined the track team and become class president.

Yuzuru Takeshita, July 1941

Yuzuru and his best friend there, Tsugio Inoue, studied for their middle-school entrance exams together and dreamed about joining the Japanese navy. When his middle-school teacher told Yuzuru he couldn't join the military because he wasn't a Japanese citizen, he was upset. Despite this disappointment, he was happy living in Japan, but upon learning that a war between Japan and the United States might soon break out, his parents decided that he and his brother should come back to California to be with the rest of their family. It was 1940. "I did not want to leave," he wrote years later. "Besides, I had forgotten English altogether and could no longer even enjoy the Sunday comics my mother used to send to us."

It had been difficult adjusting to life in Japan when he had arrived six years earlier, and now he had to readjust all over again—this time to America, a place that no longer felt like home. Making matters worse, at fourteen years old, he had to start the third grade over again because his English had become so rusty. Yuzuru was quite unhappy about this, and adding insult to injury, his little sisters were now ahead of him in school! Smart as he was, he advanced quickly, but he was still far behind the classmates who had been his friends before he moved to Japan. By this point, they were all juniors in high school. "Once again," he recalled, "my self-esteem was at its lowest, much like it was when I first went to Japan in 1934." If Pearl Harbor had not happened, his parents told him years later, they would have likely sent him back to Japan, where he would have been happier.

But Pearl Harbor *did* happen.

"WHERE IS PEARL HARBOR?"

On Sunday morning, December 7, 1941, Yuzuru, his older brother, and some friends were at a basketball game. Halfway through the game, Yuzuru later wrote, "Someone came running into the gymnasium with copies of newspapers with huge headlines about Pearl Harbor. Stunned, we all looked at each other and asked: 'Where is Pearl Harbor?'"

The next morning, the school gathered in the auditorium to listen to President Franklin D. Roosevelt's "Day of Infamy" speech. "Suddenly, the whole school was staring at us," Yuzuru later said. "A very weird feeling. We felt very uncomfortable." He recalled, "In class and on the playground, steely eyes of our non-Japanese classmates intimidated us." A week later, his eighth-grade teacher asked any Boy Scouts who were of Japanese descent to turn in their flashlights, compasses, and pocket knives. "I suppose she feared," he later told filmmaker Ilana Sol in an interview for her documentary *On Paper Wings*, "that we might use them for sabotage . . . that we might be waiting for the right moment. It was a very scary time." In a 2002 article he wrote, Yuzuru further reflected on this affront by his teacher: "To this day, my voice breaks when I relate this ugly episode to those who seek to hear about our wartime internment experience."

There are certain dates that people never forget. For many of Japanese descent in America, February 19, 1942, is one of those dates—the day President Roosevelt issued Executive Order 9066. It had been just over a year since the Takeshita brothers had returned to California. Overnight, Yuzuru, now a fifteen-year-old American teenager, was not safe in his own country. And within three months, like many other families, the Takeshitas were forced to leave their home.

The Takeshita family burned any items that could be considered pro-Japanese. Yuzuru later wrote they were told to get rid of anything "suggesting pro-Japan sentiments such as any family photos containing anyone in Japanese military uniform, books, magazines, and records that had any martial flavor to them, and, of course, any equipment such as a short-wave radio, torch light, or arms—whether operational or not—that may be construed as potential weapons for use in any subversive acts." What they couldn't burn, they buried in their backyard.

On May 9, Yuzuru filled the one suitcase he was allotted with his English and Japanese dictionaries, making room for those precious possessions by layering as much of his clothing on his body as possible. "*Shikata ga nai*," many Japanese parents told their children. Translation? "It can't be helped."

But, in a larger sense, it *could* have been helped. Many of these people were American citizens being forced from their own homes and herded off by the thousands like criminals. And the ones who weren't American citizens hadn't done anything to deserve such terrible treatment, either.

First, the Takeshita family was put on a bus and sent to an "assembly center" that had been hastily set up on the Tanforan Racetrack near the

Like the Takeshita family, this family in Hayward, California, was transferred by bus to the Tanforan Assembly Center.

San Francisco International Airport. These "assembly centers" were temporary while the WRA was readying the ten "relocation centers," where the approximately 120,000 people would eventually be housed. Tanforan was only about twenty minutes from the Takeshitas' house. Can you imagine how scary and surreal it would feel to be so close to home but have no idea what was going to happen to you or where you were going to end up?

The Tanforan Assembly Center, in San Bruno, California. The barracks for family living quarters typically had a door that opened into two small rooms. Photo by Dorothea Lange.

When the family arrived at Tanforan, people were assigned to make-shift barracks. "Because we were a family of ten," Yuzuru's younger brother Ben recounted in an article more than seventy years later, "we were fortunate to get the jockeys' barracks inside the racetrack. But my cousin's family of four were assigned to the horse stables. I would go visit them, and I can still smell the stench of horse manure to this day." The Takeshita family had two rooms for all of them to share. They were given large canvas bags and told to gather and stuff hay in the bags, to use as their mattresses. Thankfully, their mother had brought some pillows and blankets with them.

The walls in the barracks, which were open at the top, were made of thin plywood, and voices carried. The shocking difference between the comforts of home and the harsh reality of this situation was immediately apparent. "There was no running water, so we had to walk to the latrines outside, and the only light was one bulb hanging down from the ceiling on a wire. There was a total lack of privacy, especially in the latrines, no partitions between toilets or showers. The men and boys got used to it, but my sisters were very shocked," Ben remembered. He was eleven at the time.

Their first day at Tanforan, Yuzuru learned that any Japanese books would be confiscated, so he snuck out of the barracks late that night, crept under one of the buildings, and hid his dictionaries there. "I was not going to let the authorities deny me my right to study the two lan-guages, English and Japanese, that represent my dual heritage." The fam-ily was kept at the "assembly center" for four months. They made the best of a bad situation, making new friends with other young people they met at Tanforan.

At the time this photo was taken, Tanforan had been open for only two days, as busload after busload of people arrived. These newly arrived detainees are lining up at the one open mess hall, or eating area, for lunch. The wide road running diagonally across the photograph is the former racetrack. Photo by Dorothea Lange.

On the Fourth of July, an Independence Day celebration was held. The irony was thick. Yuzuru later reflected on his own personal triumph that day. A strong runner since his middle-school days, he chose to compete in the holiday race held on the track. Although there was stiff competition from other detainees—including a former member of the University of California, Los Angeles, track team—Yuzuru took first place.

"THE GUARDS WERE POINTING GUNS AT US"

In September 1942, the Takeshita family was transferred with other detainees on a rickety train to the Topaz Relocation Center in Utah—one of the ten "camps" that had been set up to hold the detainees. It was a very uncertain time, as they really had no way to know where they were going or what life was going to be like when they got there. Heightening this sense of unease was the fact that they were not allowed to open the window shades on the train

Ben Takeshita, one of Yuzuru Takeshita's younger brothers

car to even *see* where they were headed. Ben remembered asking one of the MPs (military police) if he could look out the window when they passed San Mateo so he could say goodbye to his home, not knowing if they were ever going to return. The MP simply said, "No." But Ben knew how many stops there were between San Francisco and San Mateo, so he cleverly counted the number of signal sounds the train made at each stop's crossing and said his own private goodbye to San Mateo as they passed.

During a scheduled stop in Salt Lake City, another train pulled up alongside theirs. It was filled with American soldiers heading off to war. Although Yuzuru prayed for their safety, the troops hollering at them out their windows behaved abominably. He later remembered it as a "humiliating experience" as they were "greeted with abusive catcalls and obscene gestures." Still, in his generous heart, he hoped those soldiers would survive their deployment.

When the MP finally told them they could open the window shades, there was nothing to see but dirt and dust. Located in the Sevier Desert in central Utah, Topaz was dubbed "the Whirlwind Valley." The fine sand would get whipped up by the wind, stinging people's skin and seeping through cracks in windows and walls. Most of the detainees were from the San Francisco area, and it was a much different climate from what they were used to. Summer temperatures were often over 100 degrees, and there were no trees for shade or respite from the heat. Winters were frigid, with temperatures below zero. The Takeshita family saw their first snowfall there.

Topaz had only recently been opened, and parts of it were still being

Topaz Relocation Center barracks, Topaz, Utah

built. Many of the detainees helped with construction and landscaping. Of the nearly twenty thousand acres that made up the Topaz Relocation Center, 640 acres were devoted to living space. There were thirty-four residential "blocks," each able to house 250 to 300 people. Topaz averaged about eight thousand people at any given time. Each block had twelve barracks, made from pine boards covered with tar paper. A layer of drywall on the inside provided some protection from the elements. Barracks were furnished with army cots and potbellied stoves. There was no running water. Each block had a dining ("mess") hall and a building equipped with toilets, washrooms, and a laundry room.

Topaz was still under construction when it opened. Here, detainees have volunteered to work on the interior of one of the barracks.

As at Tanforan, they made the best of things. Ben later described how he saw things as a kid: "We knew we were confined in this prison and the guards were pointing guns at us, but we couldn't do anything about it. So we did our best to survive and enjoy life as best we could. We played marbles [he had managed to smuggle his bag of marbles from home], and the older kids formed teams and played against the other blocks, mostly softball."

Yuzuru was able to finish junior high while at Topaz and excel in his classes. On June 12, 1943, among a class of 150 students, he was asked to be one of the main speakers at the graduation ceremony. He called his speech "Plans for the Future" and talked about "being optimistic about

Yuzuru's junior high graduation at Topaz; he is sitting second from left.

our future in spite of the setback we had suffered from our internment." He also said he had "faith in our American system and keeping hopes high in adversity." This was quite remarkable, for several reasons. Yuzuru had a complex relationship with the concept of democracy, as his understanding of it was influenced by his years growing up in Japan *and* America. In Japan, he had learned that democracy was not a system worth modeling. Back in America, at first he had met the forced removal orders with a certain amount of inevitability, in keeping with the phrase *Shikata ga nai*. But his eighth-grade civics class at Topaz piqued his curiosity and caused him to examine the ideals of democracy further. This study was what fueled those words he wrote in his graduation speech.

Yuzuru stayed at Topaz until September, when he was involuntarily moved again. This time, he was sent back to California, to the Tule Lake Relocation Center, in Newell, just south of the Oregon border. Tule Lake was the biggest and worst of the ten camps. It was designed to hold twelve thousand people, but by the previous September, its numbers had grown to more than fifteen thousand. Additional barracks continued to be added to accommodate all the people who were being sent there, and at its peak, there were nearly nineteen thousand people detained at Tule Lake. Seventeen-year-old Yuzuru—and the rest of his large ten-member family—were among them. At least they were still all together.

But why were the Takeshitas sent there?

"NO-NOS"

In January 1943, anyone of Japanese descent who was seventeen or older—the legal age to serve in the US military—was required to answer a questionnaire. This questionnaire was designed to find out who among the detainees would be allowed to leave, as well as who was willing to serve in the US military and therefore loyal to America (even though many of them had already been turned away when trying to register at the beginning of the war).

Let's rest there for a moment.

The War Department wanted to know how many people, *who were being held against their will by their own government*, were willing to leave their lives behind and fight for that same government in the war.

In history books, we sometimes skim past a perhaps seemingly dry fact like this questionnaire. But documents affect the lives of real human beings. To get a sense of how thousands and thousands of people were impacted by what became known as the loyalty questionnaire, let's look at the Takeshita family as a typical example.

The Takeshita family in July 1941. Back row, left to right: Ben, Spencer, Yuzuru, Roy, Kyoko. Front row, left to right: Setsuko, Manzo (their father), Michiko, Hatsumi (their mother); on her lap is Yoshio.

The Takeshita family included two parents—both of whom were Issei, or Japanese-born immigrants. They emigrated to the United States and, under laws specifically aimed at the Japanese, were not allowed to become citizens or buy (or even lease) property. Those parents had eight children, all of whom were Nisei, which means they were born in the country their parents emigrated to. This also means that all eight of them were US citizens. Like other families, their first priority above all else was to stay together—and there was a real fear that their answers to the questionnaire could break them apart.

With that brief background in mind, let's look at the questions themselves. While most of them were fairly straightforward, some were pretty private, such as disclosing details of foreign investments, names of magazines or newspapers subscribed to, and knowledge of foreign languages (although *only* Japanese was listed as a choice). Questions 27 and 28, though, were decidedly tricky, worded with loaded language that had people struggling to know how to answer without further jeopardizing their already uncertain futures. Here are those questions:

Question 27: Are you willing to serve in the armed forces of the United States on combat duty, wherever ordered?

Question 28: Will you swear unqualified allegiance to the United States of America and faithfully defend the United States from any and all attack from foreign or domestic forces, and forswear any form of allegiance or obedience to the Japanese emperor, or any other foreign government, power, or organization?

By 1900, fewer than twenty-five thousand Japanese had emigrated to the United States. But in the next twenty-five years, more than one hundred thousand had. Although that was a tiny percentage of the US population, the backlash had begun, and exclusionary laws were put into place. Many Issei got around the land laws by buying or leasing land in the names of their American-born children.

Now back to the Takeshita family. Yuzuru's older brother Spencer, like many others, was upset because he felt the questionnaire was crafted to label people disloyal—people who had *already* been labeled "alien enemies" by their government. Spencer started visiting the mess halls at Topaz, discouraging people from answering yes to these two questions or encouraging them not to answer the questions at all. Why?

Look at Question 27 again: *Are you willing to serve in the armed forces of the United States on combat duty, wherever ordered?* If either of their parents answered yes to this question, they would run the risk of having to leave their young children behind to be sent abroad to serve in a war. That wasn't something either of them could agree to do. The two oldest brothers could, theoretically, agree to fight. It would, they knew, "prove" their loyalty to the United States. But how was that even a fair question to ask of people who had been kept prisoner by their own government? Throughout the camps, there were also rumors circulating that perhaps the questionnaire was a way the US government had decided to get rid of them—by sending them off to combat duty to die in the war.

Question 28 was worse. To forswear something means to give it up or to do without it. Therefore, answering yes to a question asking if they would "forswear any form of allegiance or obedience to the Japanese emperor" would mean that a person once *had* allegiance to the Japanese emperor. Put a different way, answering yes was synonymous with claiming previous loyalty to Japan. To most Nisei like Spencer and Yuzuru, answering yes to Question 28 might also have seemed ridiculous—born in America, what would Nisei know of the Japanese emperor? For Issei like their parents, answering yes to Question 28 would make them disloyal to two countries in one fell swoop, leaving them with no country at all. That is never safe.

That is why every Takeshita family member of eligible age to take the questionnaire answered no and no to Questions 27 and 28.

Now, you might be thinking, given the breakdown you just read, that most people taking the questionnaire answered similarly. But that was not the case. As logical as it may seem in hindsight, fear was the driving factor that made most people answer yes and yes, despite the fact that their answers weren't likely true. And the government seemed to be banking on that fear—testing the loyalty of an already vulnerable and disenfranchised group of people who were afraid to appear disloyal. In the end, the yeses were, so to speak, rewarded.

The Takeshitas had answered no, ultimately, to keep their family together. That part of the strategy worked. But the people who answered yes were released from the detention centers much earlier than those who answered no. The Takeshitas—like the nearly ten thousand other "No-Nos," as they were called—were labeled disloyal and un-American, and were moved to Tule Lake.

A TEEN AT TULE LAKE

Once again, the detainees had no idea what fate would hold for them once they got to their destination. In preparation for receiving the new influx of detainees, Tule Lake was converted into a maximum-security facility complete with army tanks, seven-foot-high barbed-wire fences, and twenty-eight guard towers. The reality was clear. They were prisoners.

The "disloyal" label did not fade easily. In the government's eyes, and indeed among the Japanese community who had answered yes, many No-Nos felt like they were trying to shake a shadow. Ben Takeshita talked about this in an interview in 2019. He graduated from high school five years after the war ended, in 1950—just in time for the Korean War to have started. He said, "I didn't want that stigma to be hanging on all over me for the rest of my life, so I felt that this would be a good opportunity for me to prove my loyalty as a person, so I joined the US Army."

A detained family in their Tule Lake barracks. This is an example of a typical apartment and shows the homemade furniture and other accessories used to create some small sense of comfort.

There were all kinds of rumors circulating within Tule Lake, including the idea that people might be sent to Japan in exchange for American prisoners of war or simply deported there. Amid such uncertainty, it seemed important that the primarily English-speaking Nisei make sure they had decent Japanese-language skills. Many Issei parents also wanted their American-born children to affirm their cultural heritage, no matter where they ended up once they were released. So several Japanese-language schools were established at Tule Lake. Spencer (who was bilingual) and some of his friends started one of them, and he made sure his younger siblings attended. Five days a week, Nisei at Tule Lake studied Japanese language, as well as Japanese history and geography. The WRA condoned these schools, but the situation was not without tension.

Yuzuru attended these classes, but he also chose to enroll in Tule Lake's Tri-State High School. Partly because of the rumors that people labeled disloyal might be deported to Japan, Yuzuru reasoned it would be smart to continue improving his English as much

Despite the situation, Yuzuru busied himself with his own growth as a student and had a meaningful high school experience, which was particularly influenced by teacher Margaret Gunderson.

as possible. He even imagined, if it came to being deported, that he might someday become a diplomat as a means of working for ways to make peace between America and Japan. As it turned out, his choice to attend Tri-State High was a life-changing one. There, he met Margaret Gunderson.

Before the war, Gunderson had been a high school English and history teacher in San Leandro, California, coincidentally quite near where Yuzuru had grown up. Her husband, Martin, was the superintendent of schools.

They had a lot of Japanese American students, and as they started to lose them to the incarceration, they felt compelled to do something. As a protest, they both resigned from their jobs to teach at Tule Lake so they could help make sure a proper education was being provided for the people who were being treated so abominably by their own nation. The Gundersons paid their own price for this choice. Some of the townspeople who lived near Tule Lake treated them as traitors, and they had trouble getting any service at stores and restaurants when they went into town. The Gundersons considered it a small consequence.

Margaret Gunderson's compassion and teaching skills impacted the lives of many high school students at Tule Lake, several of whom kept in touch with her for decades.

Margaret Gunderson's arrival made an indelible impression on Yuzuru from her very first day. "In high school," he later wrote, "we were a rebellious bunch, confused and angered by what was perceived to be a betrayal of an implicit trust we had in the system." But Gunderson emphasized that while what was happening to them was in violation of their constitutional rights, it was important to recognize that it wasn't the fault of the Constitution itself; instead, it was the fault of the political leadership on the West Coast and in Washington, DC.

What may have made an even bigger impact on Yuzuru was Gunderson discussing with her students the necessity of citizens not standing by and letting unjust things happen without speaking up for equality and justice. "Americans are not perfect," he remembered her saying, "but we must never forget that democracy is a difficult journey, not a destination already reached." She told them they must fight for the rights of every citizen, no matter their ethnic or racial background.

For Yuzuru, these daylight hours spent in school helped make the rest of the time in the barracks more bearable. He would hold that experience close for the rest of his life, reflecting that "in those darkest hours of our lives, Mrs. Gunderson lifted us out of the abyss of disillusionment and despair, and presented us a challenge and a goal worth striving for as American citizens."

Yuzuru's incarceration experience could easily have resulted in his losing faith in democracy altogether, but in part because of Gunderson's influence, instead he grew to champion it, even while living under the extreme circumstances of his incarceration. "Like any other American high school boy," he later wrote, "I read and was inspired by Thomas Jefferson, the Constitution, the Atlantic Charter, etc., but in a high school surrounded by barbed-wire fences and guarded by American soldiers with

One of the Tule Lake barracks being used as a temporary high school in 1942. The school had not yet been named; posters with possible choices are tacked around the door.

machine guns. The authorities wanted us to believe that they were protecting us from possible attack from the 'outside,' but I remember how those machine guns were pointed at us!" It was obvious to him that protection was not part of his captors' goals just from the design of the fences. "The top of the barbed-wire fences was turned inward, to keep us in," he later recalled, "not to keep outsiders out."

Even so, inspired by Gunderson's teachings, Yuzuru wrote a book report on Thomas Jefferson's respect for democracy. The day he shared the report in class, there happened to be a visitor in the room. Dillon S. Myer, the new director of the WRA, listened intently and was moved to tears by Yuzuru's words. (Myer had replaced Milton Eisenhower, who had resigned just three months into his appointment, apparently quite troubled by the position, which he had reluctantly agreed to take on in the first place.) Before Myer left the class, he approached the teen and shook his hand, saying "how touched he was to witness an expression of faith in our American system by one betrayed by it."

You might imagine how conflicting this all was for Yuzuru. As he later wrote, "These were indeed agonizing times for me as I was desperately searching for my true identity underneath the various incriminating labels slapped on me over the years."

Gunderson reflected on the young man she had come to know. Writing in his autograph book before he graduated, she said: "If you were my son, I'd be so proud that I'm sure I would burst with joy." Years after the war, she asked Yuzuru how he felt about having been a No-No. "Thank goodness I was," he told her. "I would not have met you had I not been one."

In addition to Yuzuru, Margaret Gunderson stayed in touch with a few of her other former students from Tule Lake. She died in 1997, at the age of ninety-four.

These two paintings were done by detainee George Tamura in 1944 in the sumi-e style—an ink wash technique meant to capture the essence of the subject matter. Tamura was fifteen at the time of his incarceration. His paintings were hidden away until 2004, when a research student named Kenji Liu discovered them in an unlabeled box at the National Japanese

American Historical Society. Liu noticed Tamura had made several of his small paintings on the backs of detainment notices. As Tamura said in an interview for the PBS series *History Detectives*, "It was hard to get anything in the camp there, even pieces of paper. I had to put down an image of what life was like there." Reflecting on why he hadn't painted any people, Tamura said, "It was probably because I felt that it was simply no place for people to be living."

Top: Tri-State High School and its auditorium at Tule Lake in 1944
Bottom: Barbed-wire fencing and one of the twenty-eight guard towers at Tule Lake

四
CHAPTER
FOUR

Meanwhile, far from the barbed-wire fences of Tule Lake, the United States had become fully enmeshed in World War II. Germany and Italy had declared war on the United States three days after Pearl Harbor. When the Japanese bombed Australia, the United States sent troops to help fight there. And on April 9, 1942, US and Filipino troops, fighting together against the Japanese on the Bataan Peninsula, in the Philippines, surrendered to the Japanese. The Japanese marched seventy-six thousand prisoners sixty-five miles to prison camps under harsh treatment and intense heat. Along the way, thousands died in what became known as the Bataan Death March. At least 5,200 among them were Americans.

Nine days later, on April 18, 1942, in retaliation for Pearl Harbor, the United States sent a clear message to Japan that it, too, could strike their nation on its home soil. The message came in the form of an air raid on Tokyo led by a daring pilot, Lieutenant Colonel James Doolittle, who had hatched the idea. Sixteen B-25 bomber planes, launched from a US aircraft carrier off the coast of Japan, attacked the mainland of Japan in what became known as the Doolittle Raid.

Thirteen of the bombers targeted Tokyo, with each of the three remaining planes striking Nagoya, Osaka, and Kobe. Although the damage was minimal, the psychological effect was huge. For the Americans, it was a confidence booster at a time when things weren't going their way in the Pacific fighting. For the Japanese, it was a realization that they were, in fact, vulnerable at home—something the Japanese government had promised its people they had no need to fear.

The war raged on in Europe and the Pacific. Deployed service members, Americans included, knew the horrors of war while fighting on far-flung battlefields. But even after Pearl Harbor, it is safe to say that most Americans felt fairly secure in the belief that the war was not going to stretch across the ocean to land at their feet on the continental United States.

DESIGNING NEW WEAPONS OF WAR

If you have ever flown from west to east in an airplane, it is likely you have experienced the effects of strong, high-altitude westerly winds that made your trip faster than if you had been traveling in the opposite direction. These winds are now well known and are frequently utilized by pilots to shorten travel times in the air and save fuel, and by meteorologists to predict weather patterns. (The strength of the air current actually pushes weather conditions around the world.) But during World War II, this jet stream (a term that had not yet been coined) was not common knowledge. Research done in 1926, conducted by Japanese meteorologist Wasaburo Ooishi, led to its discovery.

What exactly is the jet stream? One scientist described it as a "hose-like band of high-speed winds at high levels [that] wanders in serpentine fashion." It is essentially a river of air, flowing west to east (the same direction the Earth rotates). It exists at an altitude of about twenty thousand feet, or six to nine miles, above the surface of the Earth, near the top of the part of Earth's atmosphere called the troposphere. The jet stream can stretch thousands of miles across the globe in length, but it is not nearly as wide. In some places, the width of the jet stream is less than three miles, but it can also be as much as a few hundred miles wide. The jet stream can reach speeds up to three hundred miles per hour. Imagine the assist an airplane can receive from traveling on this current!

Science and war often go hand in hand. Governments at war utilize their scientists in all kinds of ways. Their discoveries and calculations can be used for spying or building weapons. In 1933, several years

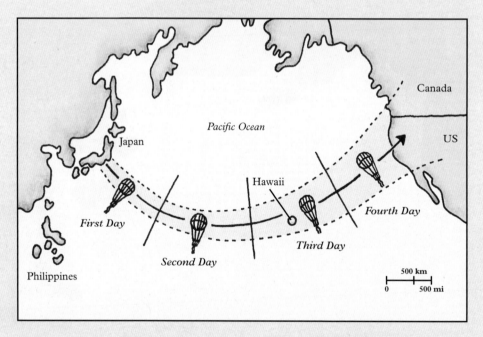

This map illustrates the concept of utilizing the force of the jet stream to carry Japanese balloon bombs across the Pacific Ocean over the course of just a few days.

after Ooishi's initial discovery, the Japanese military began the Proposed Airborne Carrier research and development program to focus on designing new weapons of war. Japanese scientists furthered Ooishi's research to see if the winds could be used for military purposes. They measured things like temperature, humidity, and wind direction.

All this knowledge would soon be put to practical use. The use of balloons to carry weapons had been attempted with limited success by the Austrians nearly one hundred years earlier. The discovery of the jet stream as a high-speed method of transport inspired these Japanese scientists to return to the idea of using balloons. They began to develop balloons of different sizes and materials to test how they might travel long distances via the jet stream and be used as effective long-range weapons carriers.

"FIND A WAY TO BOMB AMERICA"

As with most scientific endeavors, trial and error is a big part of the process. One promising project was a balloon about thirteen feet in diameter that could carry explosives. The design kept the balloon at a consistent altitude, but the maximum distance it traveled was only about seventy miles. Over the next several years, Japanese scientists experimented with different ideas, but it was more of a back-burner effort. Until the Doolittle Raid, that is.

Prime Minister Tojo and other Japanese leaders were enraged. If America was going to terrify Japanese citizens at home, Japan was going to strike back in kind. Japan vowed to hit the continental United States so Americans could feel, firsthand, the terrors of war on their home soil. "Infuriated that mainland America remained comfortably untouched, the Imperial General Headquarters demanded a retaliatory strike on the

United States. . . . A simple directive went out to scientists and engineers at the Noborito Institute. . . . Find a way to bomb America," wrote historian Ross Coen in *Fu-Go: The Curious History of Japan's Balloon Bomb Attack on America*.

Doolittle's raid didn't only trigger a swift and strong military reaction from Japan. It had a deep effect on its civilians, too. Up until this point, the Japanese people believed their homeland was invincible, that they were protected by their leaders. This faith had been wiped out. "Now things are different," Japanese ace pilot Saburo Sakai's young cousin wrote him. "Bombs have been dropped here on our homes. It does not seem anymore that there is such a great difference between the battle front and the home front."

Renewed efforts arose to test and develop an effective balloon bomb. One involved a joint project between the Japanese army and navy. A larger balloon (nearly twenty feet in diameter) was designed that could carry a time-released bomb. It was able to fly about 620 miles—but that was only one-tenth the distance needed, as approximately 6,200 miles of ocean stretched between Japan and the United States. Instead of being launched from Japan, then, this balloon would need to be launched from a submarine positioned within 620 miles off the West Coast of the United States. A couple hundred of these balloons were made, but the project was halted because the Japanese navy could no longer afford to spare any submarines for this effort.

Japanese scientists started developing a new balloon—one that would be capable of traveling all the way to the United States on its own via the jet stream. There were a lot of issues that needed ingenious solutions. The hydrogen gas used to propel the balloon would have to be able to withstand pressure and temperature changes during the course of the journey. This meant devising a way to vent the gas when it heated so that the balloon wouldn't burst. Scientists also needed to figure out how to deal with the gas contracting during cooler nighttime temperatures, which could cause the balloon to deflate and fall from the sky.

While the scientists worked on designing these systems, one of the biggest questions was whether the jet stream could even carry a balloon all the way across the ocean. To find the answer, meteorologist Hidetoshi Arakawa looked back at Ooishi's data from the early 1920s and discovered that these westerly winds were seasonal—and strongest in winter. Arakawa then did his own calculations, mapping out flow patterns that took into account data from weather stations in different parts of Japan. His work indicated that balloons launched from November to March from specific locations could cross the ocean. Balloons equipped with transmitters were then used to test the hypothesis and gather more data. Based on the percentage of balloons that continued to transmit data for the length of time it would take to cross the ocean, it was concluded that while it would likely work, only about 10 percent of the balloons would make it all the way to America. Therefore, the plan was to launch upward of ten thousand balloons!

This balloon bomb mission needed two things to succeed—a jaw-dropping number of person-hours and an enormous amount of materials to build the bombs and incendiary devices (explosives intended to set fires), as well as the balloons that would carry them. Miles and miles of fuse cords were needed, for example, as well as detonators, battery housings, and so on.

Money and resources were in short supply, so the balloons would need to be made cheaply and—perhaps more importantly—without using up invaluable materials otherwise needed for Japan's primary war efforts.

Lightweight, strong, and inexpensive Japanese paper called washi was the answer. But to make ten thousand paper balloons was a huge undertaking. Who could be used to make them?

五

CHAPTER FIVE

Fifteen-year-old Tetsuko Tanaka dreamed of becoming a ballerina. She had just started attending the Yamaguchi Girls' High School, in Yamaguchi, Japan, on the southwest side of the island of Honshu. But in her first year there, Japan had gone to war with America and Great Britain. Although courses continued, English-language classes were canceled, and no American or English music was allowed to be part of music studies. The following year, fewer and fewer classes were taught as students were called on to volunteer their time for the war effort, helping families whose sons were away from home, fighting for Japan. Tanaka's classmates spent their school hours patching soldiers' uniforms, weeding rice paddies, helping harvest crops, and generally making themselves useful. They knew it was their patriotic duty.

"I carried charcoal down from the mountains. I'd had no farm experience before. It was very strenuous, physical labor, but I never thought of it

(Above) Japanese schoolgirls work to make paper balloons in a factory during World War II.

as hardship," Tanaka said. "Nobody complained about it. We were part of a divine country centered on the Emperor. The whole Japanese race was fighting a war."

This matter-of-fact attitude was grounded in the reality that Japan was governed by military rule. Japanese children grew up understanding what was expected of them by their government. In Japan at this time, teenagers as young as fifteen were required to serve their country as soldiers. In addition, many younger schoolchildren were expected to do as they were told should the military ask for their assistance. In other words, Japanese youths understood they may be called upon to follow military orders.

And since Japan had been involved in a war with China since 1931, many Japanese children already had firsthand experience contributing to the war effort. Their patriotism as Japanese citizens was deeply engrained. As an adult, Tetsuko Tanaka looked back on that time and remembered that this was simply how growing up in Japan was. "My education stressed contributing to the war effort and being a patriot. . . . We were ordered not only to work but to lay down our lives for our country," she later said.

In August 1944, Tanaka and her classmates were recruited to make paper balloons for the military's balloon bomb project. Her school was one of many around the nation that were called upon, as thousands of Japanese high school girls were mobilized to take part in Japan's mission to attack the American mainland. Sworn to secrecy, they could not even tell their family what they were doing. Some schools, like Tanaka's, were partially transformed into makeshift factories. Other schools sent the girls to work in existing factories. If they lived nearby, they could stay at home and travel back and forth for their shifts. Otherwise, they were housed in dormitories. Conditions in the factories varied but were often dismal, with girls working grueling ten- to twelve-hour shifts.

In some locations, teenage boys were also used to make paper balloons, but the boys mobilized for the war effort were more often put to work at tasks such as digging trenches, transporting toxic material, and working in factories that produced weapons and other war supplies.

"WE PRACTICALLY STARTED A BONFIRE IN CLASS"

Reiko Okada was just thirteen when she and her classmates at Tadanoumi Girls' High School were given their mobilization orders. Her school was among seven that sent girls to the island of Ohkuno for balloon production. Ohkuno had been the location of a secret chemical weapons plant since 1929, producing poison gases and other toxic chemicals. Only people working on the island were allowed on and off. When Okada arrived, she and more than six hundred other girls received their first set of instructions. In addition to being bound to secrecy, they were told they could not bring anything off the island. Anytime they went home, they were checked to ensure that only their personal belongings went with them.

Reiko Okada's illustrative interpretation of her time on Ohkuno island making balloons for the war effort

The island was kept so secret that it was removed from all Japanese maps. The weapons plant was built at the bottom of a large hill, which kept it hidden from the mainland. Today there is a Poison Gas Museum on the site.

Making balloons was not the only task the teenagers were required to perform on Ohkuno. They also packed boxes, sealed smoke bombs, and mixed chemicals—only learning later that they had been exposed to toxic materials. There were signs and concerns that were hard to miss, though. As Okada later wrote, "Gazing at the rising moon on the way home from the island, we noticed how pathetic the blighted pine trees looked. The whole island had become polluted by the toxic gas."

Whether these girls were working in converted classrooms or gymnasiums like Tanaka or traveling to an existing factory like Okada, the balloon-making process was similar. Washi is a thin tissue-like Japanese paper made from the bark of the kozo tree, which grows all over Japan.

This illustration by Reiko Okada depicts two girls using needles from a pine tree as toothpicks, which made their mouth and gums instantly swell from the toxic gas absorbed by the needles.

Washi was the preferred paper to use for the balloons because it was both lightweight and strong. In order to make it the desired thickness for the balloon, though, several layers of washi needed to be pasted together. The paste was made from grinding konjac root—similar to potatoes—into a flour, adding water to it, and stirring for a few hours. Then two of these multilayered sheets of delicate washi—about six by three feet—were carefully laid down and glued together.

Two girls work together to make paste from konjac root.

"The girls would have to use their hands to make the paper flat and spread the konnyaku glue on them," author and historian Koichi Yoshino explained. "Much power was needed to execute this repetitive task and many of the girls would often complain about their painful bleeding fingertips after a day's work." Toshiko Inoue, a sixteen-year-old from Yame Girls' High School, remembered it well: "It was work more difficult than you could ever imagine." Each time two layers were pasted together, any little air bubbles that might have gotten trapped between the washi sheets had to be brushed out, and the sheets had to dry completely before proceeding to glue on the next layer of washi.

Toshiko Inoue; remember her name, as she factors into the story again later.

Working with washi layers at the paper drying boards

When the fall weather turned damp, the drying process slowed considerably. The pressure was on to produce the paper sheets as quickly as possible, though. At Tanaka's school, they had been working outside so the washi could dry on tables in the sun, but the rains pushed them indoors. "Eventually, we removed all the desks from the classrooms and brought in a large hibachi and a pile of charcoal," she said. "We practically started a bonfire in class, all the windows and halls lined with drying boards. Sometimes you almost got poisoned by carbon monoxide."

"PLEASE LET US GO AND SERVE THE NATION"

At the largest factory, the Kokura Arsenal, in Tokyo, things were being done on a grander scale. Tanaka and her classmates heard that girls from another high school nearby had been sent there. They wanted to go too, acutely aware, as she said, that "the war situation was intensifying. . . . We knew that if we stayed at school, production would remain low or decline, so we addressed a petition to our principal. . . . [W]e cut our fingers to write in blood, 'Please let us go and serve the nation.'"

On a cold January day in 1945, the girls got their wish. Snow fell, swirling in the wind. The mood at the Kokura Arsenal was fiercely patriotic. There was excitement in the air as the girls lined up alongside male recruits. Upon seeing a big, billowing balloon set up on display, Tanaka remembered, "It fired our determination." The girls wore white headbands that read STUDENT SPECIAL ATTACK FORCE, and all joined in chorus together, singing a war song—"Our Red Blood Burns." Tanaka recalled what her grandmother often told her: "You must behave like the daughter of a warrior family." But the students' enthusiasm would soon be challenged.

Tanaka later said, "I was shocked by the size of the factory. Everywhere, metal drying boards were revolving on steam-blasting machines that dried them. The noise was deafening." After a cold night in a dormitory with no heat, the girls were awakened at 4:30 a.m. for breakfast, then left at 5:00 a.m. to walk nearly an hour in four uniform lines to reach the factory, where they had morning assembly. "At six o'clock," Tanaka said, "we relieved the shift that had been on duty through the night."

The environment inside the factory was extremely dank and dark, with large black drapes blocking the outside light to maintain secrecy. The heat was oppressive. "The floor was muddy with the extra paste that always streamed off the drying boards," Tanaka said. "From above, steam, condensed into water droplets[,] fell on us. Each person was in charge of two drying boards. The paper dried very quickly, so you shuttled back and forth between them like a crab. If it got too dry then it would crack and fail the quality test. That was unforgivable, so we ran barefoot across the pasty floor." Many of the girls suffered fungal infections on their feet from the muck on the floor.

Once the five-layer sheets were finished, it was time for inspection. The sheets were carried into another room and meticulously checked for air bubbles. "Here, a girl would have to mount every piece of paper on a light board, bending over it for hours," Yoshino explained. "Failing to correct these imperfections would result in the hydrogen seeping through and causing the balloon to explode immediately." When an air bubble was found, it was gently opened with a pin and sealed with a bit of the konnyaku glue. Then a small patch of paper was ironed onto the spot.

Tears and weak spots were also identified with the light board. These were marked with a red pencil and underwent two stages of repair. The

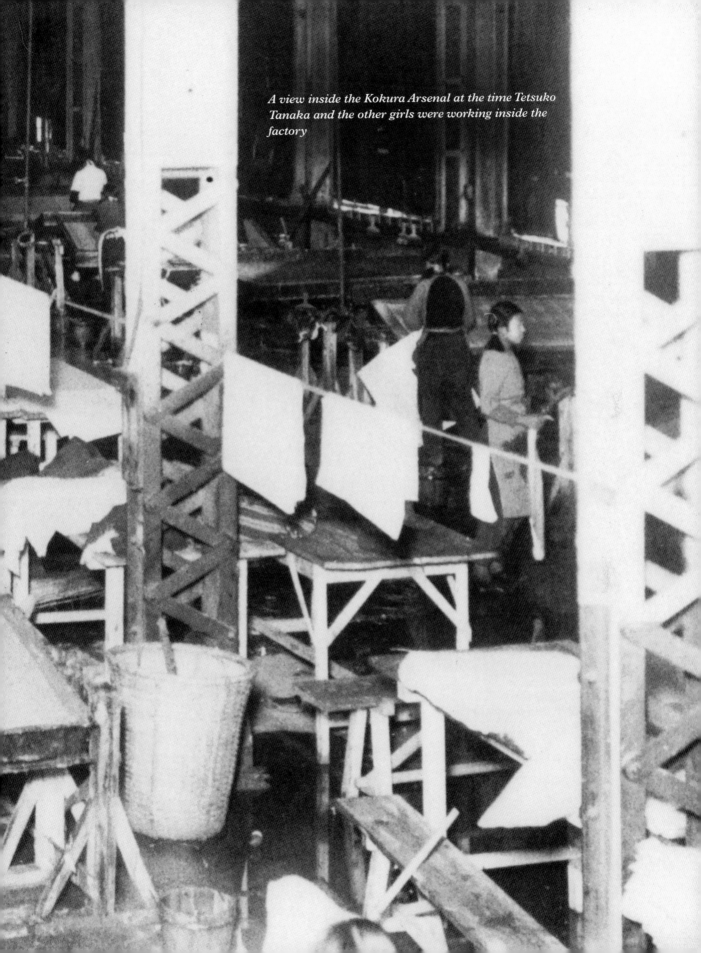

A view inside the Kokura Arsenal at the time Tetsuko Tanaka and the other girls were working inside the factory

first stage involved pasting small pieces of paper on top of those spots to reinforce them. Once all the air bubbles, tears, and weak spots had been repaired, the paper was put in a solution that dissolves bark fibers without weakening the finished paper. From there, it went into a large vat of glycerin for fifteen minutes. This made the paper more flexible and less prone to cracking. The final step—after checking again for any flaws in the paper—was to waterproof it with a coat of lacquer.

Once the paper was ready, girls who worked in the assembly room would measure and cut it into twenty-six-foot-long trapezoidal panels. It took more than five hundred of these panels to make one balloon. In order to not tear the paper, the girls' fingernails needed to be kept closely trimmed, and they were not allowed to wear hairpins. The process of assembling the panels differed depending on the size of the factory, with some of the girls reporting that panels were pasted together at the seams, while others were sewn. Two halves—or hemispheres—were made (the hemispheres were later joined to make the sphere-shaped balloon). Then more lacquer was layered for further waterproofing.

Around the balloon's center line—or equator—a fringe curtain was attached. Nineteen shroud lines would be hung from that curtain. Those lines are what would later carry the complex structure that housed the bombs and incendiary devices. The rest of the balloon bomb assembly generally did not involve the girls, but they were often present for the inflation tests.

Mending imperfections in the paper

These two Reiko Okada illustrations capture the balloon-making process.

Two girls check paper for imperfections on the light boards while two others carry washi sheets into another room to be repaired.

Girls working in a row create one half, or hemisphere, of a balloon.

For these tests, completed balloons were carefully moved into areas large enough to inflate them. Barometers measured the pressure inside the balloon. If nothing happened after twenty minutes of inflation, the test was a success. This often prompted some of the girls to shout "Banzai!" If the test discovered air leaks, though, you could hear the exasperation in their cries. Failure was crushing. They had worked too hard, given up too much.

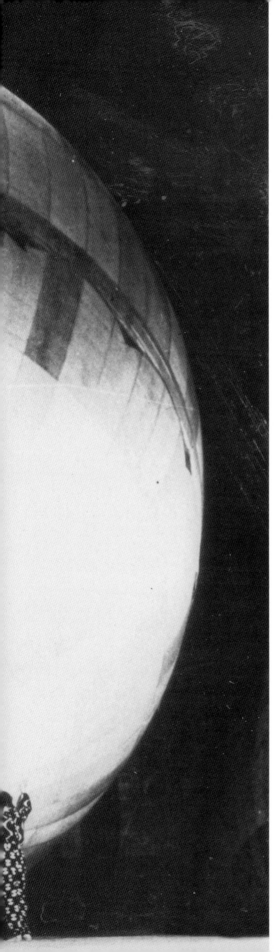

"SEASONED WITH SALT FROM MY TEARS"

"I can't recall ever eating lunch," Tanaka said. "When we returned to our dorm, we gulped down our food, little as it was. . . . We had sweet potatoes that were sometimes old and had turned black and smelled strange mixed in with rice. You got one rice bowl full of that and one cup of miso soup, nothing added. No vegetables, nothing. It wasn't enough food to sustain us at the work we had to do."

Like many other family members, Tanaka's mother couldn't visit—she was at home with four younger children, and travel priority on the trains was given to soldiers. She was able to send a neighbor with food for her daughter, though. "My mother gave her sweet bean cakes for me. I was so happy that I still remember the taste of them," Tanaka said fifty years later, "seasoned with salt from my tears."

Whether they were enduring extreme heat in the factory or bitter cold in the dormitories, working to the point of exhaustion so that they—as Tanaka put it—"slept like corpses" on their Sundays off, or tackling their duties despite extreme hunger, these teenage girls suffered enormously in the name of patriotism.

Japanese girls stand at the base of an inflated balloon. This image was likely taken during the last stage of production, in which they would have painted on lacquer to waterproof the balloon. It shows the scale of the balloon's size.

• • •

Once Japan was ready to launch its balloon bombs, the Special Balloon Regiment was formed to set up the gas facilities needed to power the balloons, train personnel to launch the balloons, and determine the best launching sites. Three were chosen to be ideally positioned along the coastline of the island of Honshu—at Otsu, Ichinomiya, and Nakoso. These sites were thought to provide the best chance for the balloons to reach the western coast of the United States. The Special Balloon Regiment had three battalions—the First Battalion was positioned at Otsu, which served as command headquarters and was 1,500 people strong. The Second Battalion, at Ichinomiya, had seven hundred personnel, and the Third Battalion, at Nakoso, had six hundred.

Every single one of those individuals was necessary because the plan to launch ten thousand balloons would take anywhere from thirty to sixty minutes per balloon—and thirty men to get each one off the ground! Working at full capacity, this translated into a maximum total launch of two hundred balloons per day, and there was only about a five-month window of time during which the jet-stream winds would be strong enough to carry the balloons across the Pacific. Meanwhile, the conditions on the ground also needed to be favorable. Too much wind, rain, or snow would hinder their attempts. It was a huge undertaking. Just the process of filling the balloons with hydrogen gas was daunting. Over the next several months, though, Japan succeeded at sending more than nine thousand balloons on their way, carrying deadly payloads.

(Right) A Japanese balloon bomb in flight over the Pacific Ocean

六
CHAPTER SIX

The first report of a strange balloon sighting occurred on November 4, 1944, when a US Navy ship pulled the remains of one from the water sixty-six miles from San Pedro, California. Ten days later, five miles off the coast of Kailua, Hawaii, the US Coast Guard found a paper balloon and some of its rigging. On December 6, many eyewitnesses in Thermopolis, Wyoming, reported hearing an explosion and seeing a bright-red flame, while others saw what they believed might have been a parachutist escaping from a crashed plane. But fairly extensive searching turned up no plane and no parachutist. What they did find was an area a few feet wide smelling of gunpowder and littered with scorched, shattered rocks, as well as circular bands of metal with remnants of rivets and fin-shaped, flat metal shards. On December 11, a father and son near Kalispell, Montana, contacted the US Air Force to report what they thought might be a downed

(Above) This demonstration photograph shows a bomb apparatus exploding.

<u>TREMONTON, UTAH, BALLOON</u>

Balloon found 23 February 1945. Partially inflated envelope showing shroud line
attachment to catenary band.

parachute near their worksite. It was not clear what any of these objects were. Radio or meteorological equipment? Weather balloons?

In the first two weeks of January 1945, more balloons were found. One of them got tangled in electrical lines at a nuclear plant in Hanford, Washington, causing a power outage. Meanwhile, the Kalispell evidence was confirmed to be a balloon, not a parachute, and Japanese writing was detected on some of the paper it was made from. More alarmingly, further investigation conducted on the metal fragments from Thermopolis identified them as pieces of a bomb likely manufactured in Japan.

Early theories started to develop that perhaps these balloons were being launched from Japanese submarines positioned off the coast. But the

Recovered near Davis, California, March 1945, this balloon was nearly intact (you can see the bomb apparatus dangling off the right side of the telephone pole). It was extremely helpful in reconstructing a complete balloon to study how they were made.

The Hanford nuclear plant was manufacturing plutonium for the atomic bomb that the United States later dropped on Nagasaki, Japan, in August 1945. If the balloon bomb had gone off, it could have triggered a nuclear explosion.

findings from Thermopolis and Kalispell prompted investigators to take a second look at the balloon that had been stuck in storage after being hauled out of the water near San Pedro, as well as the one recovered from the ocean off Kailua, Hawaii. What they discovered was a complex mechanism possibly capable of carrying balloons long distances, across the Pacific.

Soon, there were more sightings, in Oregon, Wyoming, Washington, Alaska, western Canada, and northern Mexico. And then, near Sebastopol, California, in the middle of a farmer's apple orchard, a balloon crashed down with four unexploded incendiary bombs still attached. The colonel who examined it said, flat out, "That mechanism is not a weather apparatus."

The military needed to figure out—fast—where these balloon bombs were coming from!

"AN INGENIOUS MENACE"

Forensics uses scientific techniques and tests to find evidence to solve crimes. Forensic geology—which was relatively new in 1945—finds evidence from materials in the earth to solve crimes. One of the first things recovered from the sites where balloon bombs had been found were small piles of sand, as well as some sand-filled bags—later known to be part of the system that regulated the altitude of a balloon. That sand turned out to be the key to solving the mystery of where the balloons were being launched from.

The United States Geological Survey's Military Geology Unit (MGU) was called in to analyze the sand. The MGU's forensic geologists knew right away that the sand wasn't from continental North America or Hawaii. They were also sure it had come from a beach. Microscopic studies showed tiny skeletons of foraminifera species only known to have been found on beaches on the eastern shore of the Japanese island of Honshu. Bingo! Further examination of trace minerals in the sand, combined with cross-referencing Japanese geologic studies, allowed them to pinpoint that the sand was from one of two beaches—Shiogama or Ichinomiya, Japan.

The case was quickly mounting that the Japanese had launched an offensive attack. There was speculation as to the exact purpose of these balloons and more questions than answers: Did the balloons constitute potential chemical or biological warfare? Were they carrying explosive bombs or some unknown experiment? Were they anti-aircraft devices, a distraction, or a terror technique?

There was no time to waste. Defense strategies were put into place. Air force and navy pilots were sent to shoot down sighted balloons. Smoke jumpers from the 555th Infantry Battalion and the US Forest Service were mobilized to put out fires and disarm any bombs found. Although it was later known that none of the fires put out in those areas that summer were started by the balloons, some of the 555th reported interacting with some bombs from the balloons. JJ Corbett remembered, "We found a bomb that had not detonated—it was still hanging in the brush on its balloon. So we were trained in dealing [with] and disposing of the bombs." The military looked for ways to detect and intercept balloons by radar, and the navy paid attention to any odd signals

JJ Corbett was a proud member of the 555th Infantry, aka the Triple Nickles, the first Black paratroopers in World War II. They were sent on a mission to Oregon and California to train as smokejumpers and assist the US Forest Service during the summer of 1945.

Although there is no proof that the balloons might have been used to carry biological weapons, the leader of the balloon bomb project, Major General Sueki Kusaba, apparently later admitted that Japan did have plans for utilizing the balloons for biological warfare but that he was directed to stop that plan by an unnamed superior. Speculation suggests that that superior may have been the emperor.

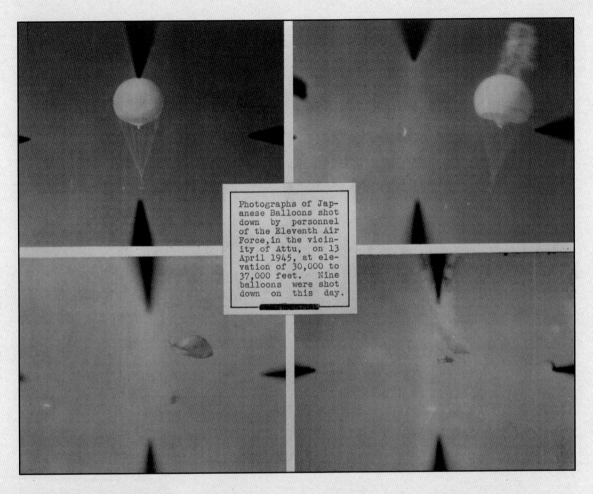

Photographs of Japanese Balloons shot down by personnel of the Eleventh Air Force, in the vicinity of Attu, on 13 April 1945, at elevation of 30,000 to 37,000 feet. Nine balloons were shot down on this day.

Even though nearly five hundred aircraft were sent to shoot down the balloons between September 1944 and December 1945, they were rarely successful. In February 1945, a fighter pilot in a P-38 shot one down over Calistoga, California. Another was shot down by the Royal Canadian Air Force in British Columbia and landed in Washington State. Another fighter pilot took one out at twelve thousand feet over North Bend, Oregon. The next month, March 1945, a balloon was taken down after fighter pilots trailed it from Oregon to Nevada, with one pilot even landing and continuing the chase in his car, to no avail! Finally, a different pilot, in a Bell P-63, succeeded—but only after the balloon had already dropped some of its payload and started to descend. The most fruitful instance occurred in April 1945 when the Eleventh Air Force managed to shoot down nine balloons over Massacre Bay on Attu Island, Alaska.

from radio transmitters. Whenever possible, materials were collected and analyzed. All in all, there were 120 balloon recoveries, thirty-two of which still had the bombs attached. This gave the military the opportunity to discover how this ingenious device was made.

Here is some of what was learned: The balloon bag itself was about thirty-two feet in diameter. It contained about nineteen thousand cubic feet of hydrogen gas. Encircling the bottom third of the balloon was a suspension curtain, from which hung shroud lines forty to fifty feet long. The shroud lines gathered at the bottom, suspending the bomb device and its components. Those components included a power source in the form of a battery (encased in three boxes, one of which was filled with a solution to protect it from freezing at night or overheating during the day); fuses,

Navy personnel steady the mechanism of an intact balloon bomb, as they ready it for examination and testing. The main bomb is suspended in the center, and a ballast sandbag hangs on the right.

At first, it was suspected the solution could contain pathogens for biological warfare, so the liquid, still in the clear box, was shipped in a lead-lined box to be tested.

plugs, and switches; a demolition block; supports to suspend the ballasts (sandbags); two to four incendiary devices (intended to set fires); the central bomb, or payload; and aneroid barometers (instruments that measure pressure without using liquid), each set to specific altitudes for triggering the ballasts—and eventually the bomb—to drop.

This system of triggers was clever and complex. The way the balloons had been designed to travel was carefully timed and mapped out according to changes in altitude, wind speed, and distance. After initial launch, the balloons would quickly ascend to altitudes of over thirty thousand feet, but without a system to control their flight, they would have eventually just lost altitude. The documentary *On a Wind and a Prayer* describes the process well: "After one hour, the launching fuse, pulled at launch, would burn out, thus arming the first ballast plugs. The master aneroid was now also activated, and in control of its flight. As the balloon's journey continued, it reached its first night cycle and would start to lose its buoyancy. As it descended by some 2,700 feet, the master aneroid would establish an electric contact, causing the ballasting plugs to blow. By dropping the first of its many sandbags, the balloon was able to rise back up to its operating altitude." This process was done in sequence and repeated itself over the next few days and nights. If all went well, by the fourth day, the balloons would have successfully floated across the Pacific Ocean.

Then, after the last sandbag had been let loose, the payload would be dropped. The rest of the device was designed to self-destruct. No longer weighed down by its payload, the balloon bag would float up to a higher altitude, where a magnesium flare would ignite the flammable hydrogen inside the balloon and the remaining evidence would explode. When this all occurred as planned, the payloads made it to their destinations.

This balloon was recovered and inflated in order to study it. The structure of a cloth skirt with shroud lines attached to it can be clearly seen.

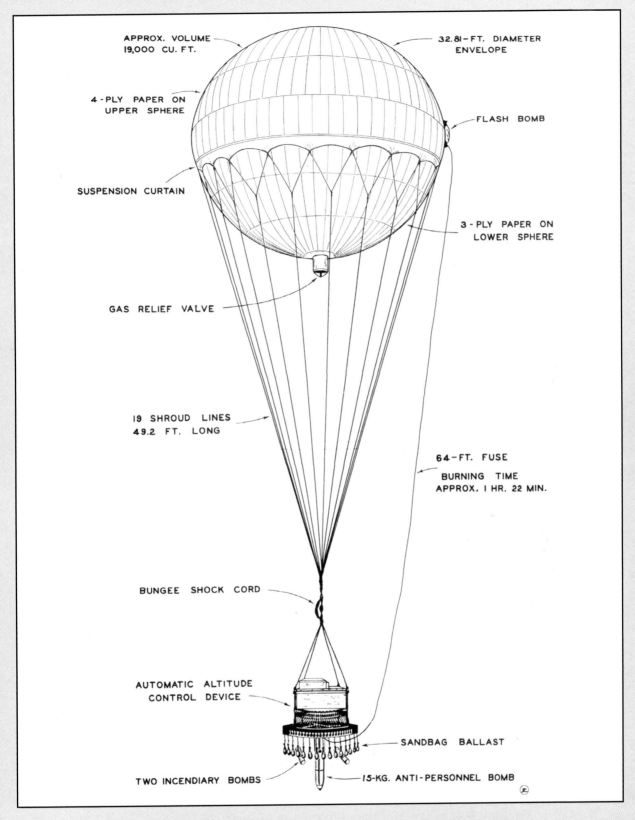

APPROX. VOLUME
19,000 CU. FT.

32.81 - FT. DIAMETER
ENVELOPE

4 - PLY PAPER ON
UPPER SPHERE

FLASH BOMB

SUSPENSION CURTAIN

3 - PLY PAPER ON
LOWER SPHERE

GAS RELIEF VALVE

19 SHROUD LINES
49.2 FT. LONG

64 - FT. FUSE
BURNING TIME
APPROX. 1 HR. 22 MIN.

BUNGEE SHOCK CORD

AUTOMATIC ALTITUDE
CONTROL DEVICE

SANDBAG BALLAST

TWO INCENDIARY BOMBS

15 - KG. ANTI - PERSONNEL BOMB

*Meticulous diagrams of the Japanese balloon bomb design were created by
Robert Mikesh, who became one of the world's authorities on this weapon.*

A photograph of the intact bomb apparatus taken before the demonstration explosion shown on page 74

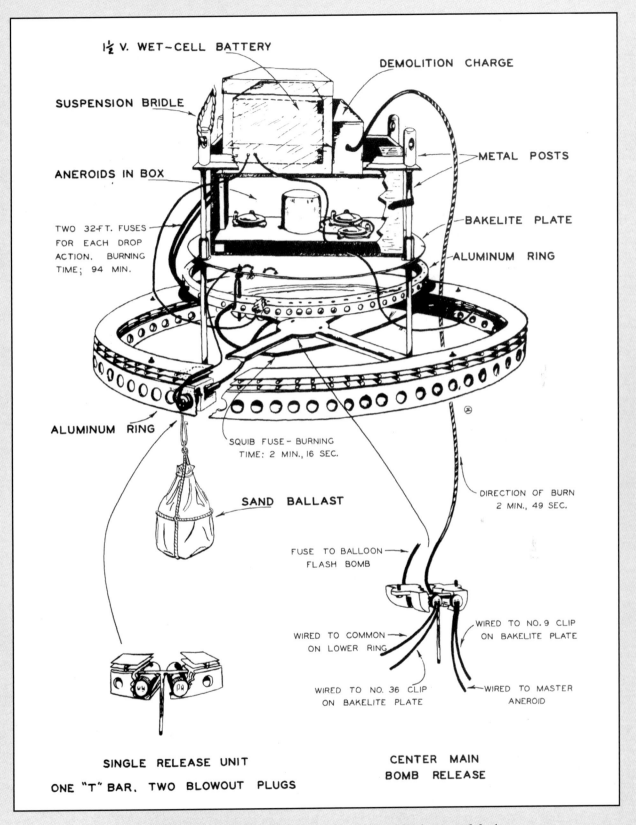

1½ V. WET–CELL BATTERY

DEMOLITION CHARGE

SUSPENSION BRIDLE

METAL POSTS

ANEROIDS IN BOX

BAKELITE PLATE

ALUMINUM RING

TWO 32-FT. FUSES FOR EACH DROP ACTION. BURNING TIME; 94 MIN.

ALUMINUM RING

SQUIB FUSE - BURNING TIME: 2 MIN., 16 SEC.

SAND BALLAST

DIRECTION OF BURN 2 MIN., 49 SEC.

FUSE TO BALLOON FLASH BOMB

WIRED TO NO. 9 CLIP ON BAKELITE PLATE

WIRED TO COMMON ON LOWER RING

WIRED TO NO. 36 CLIP ON BAKELITE PLATE

WIRED TO MASTER ANEROID

SINGLE RELEASE UNIT

CENTER MAIN BOMB RELEASE

ONE "T" BAR, TWO BLOWOUT PLUGS

This Robert Mikesh diagram depicts the automatic altitude-control device.

But only about 10 percent of them did. According to historian Robert Mikesh, this was most likely because of a flaw in the design of the ballast dropping system. "Blow plugs would fail to ignite," he explained, "fuses would not burn properly, the extreme temperatures that the balloons operated in was a major factor for these malfunctions." The Japanese had accounted for that, though. In the event that any circuit plugs malfunctioned during the ocean crossing, the sequence would stop, and the balloon would start to descend. At thirteen thousand feet, the payload would be dropped and a fuse would be ignited to blow the rest of the device up, keeping it from being detected.

In a long-since-declassified video made for the navy to educate personnel about the balloon bombs so they would know what to be on the lookout for, the narrator closes the training video with a dramatic statement: "Such are the facts about this ingenious menace. It may come over in larger and larger numbers. Its makeup may change. . . . Defensive measures by all services are in operation to meet this menace."

At the end of the film, the following message fills the entire screen in large bold type:

ANY BALLOONS APPROACHING THE UNITED STATES FROM OUTSIDE ITS BORDERS CAN BE ENEMY ATTACKS AGAINST THE NATION. INFORMATION THAT THE BALLOONS HAVE REACHED THIS COUNTRY, AND PARTICULARLY WHAT SECTION THEY HAVE REACHED, IS INFORMATION OF VALUE TO THE ENEMY. PLEASE DO NOT AID THE ENEMY BY PUBLISHING OR BROADCASTING OR DISCUSSING SUCH INFORMATION WITHOUT APPROPRIATE AUTHORITY.

七

CHAPTER SEVEN

One of the first and most important defense strategies put in place when the balloon sightings began involved the press—or, rather, involved keeping the news of the balloons *out* of the press. Not too surprisingly, news did slip through a few times before action was taken. The balloon spotted in Kalispell, Montana, was announced in a radio news broadcast and scrawled across a front page with a headline that read: LIFT SECRECY VEIL ON NEW ENEMY BALLOON. Ironically, the article talked about the need for secrecy, with the publisher of the paper writing, "Everybody was mighty interested, but when the Federal Bureau of Investigation warned not to discuss it, the whole town clammed up." Articles also ran in *Time* and *Newsweek*. In reaction to the press, one colonel was quoted as saying, "What's the matter with the goddamn fools? That's just like giving Tokyo a Christmas present."

And in fact, the Japanese caught wind of this first round of media and jumped on it, taking one small morsel of news and exaggerating and embellishing it to create a swirl of propaganda intended to show the Japanese people that their nation was winning and hitting America on its home turf. On February 17, 1945, Radio Tokyo broadcast the following: "Ten thousand people have been killed. One of our weapons caused great fires and damage at Kalispell, Montana. . . . Each of our secret-type balloons can carry several persons, and the day is not far distant when we will land several million Japanese troops on American soil."

Of course, this wasn't even close to true. Still, the last thing the US military wanted was for Japan to receive any more information that might show that their tactics were meeting with any success. The hope was that if Japanese military leaders thought the balloons were failing to arrive at their destination or to cause any harm when they did complete the journey, they might stop the project. Throughout the United States, the press was asked not to report any news of the balloon bomb attacks—either in print or in broadcast media. It was a matter of national security.

The press complied, as did ordinary citizens in America and Canada who experienced any sightings. They took the issue of keeping this secret quite seriously and did not spread the news. "The balloon bomb attack against North America was a real threat," Robert Mikesh explains in *On a Wind and a Prayer*. "It was actually happening. It was a matter of what is the magnitude that this was going to develop into."

Despite the hush-hush nature of the story, some rumors did start to circulate about sightings of Japanese balloon bombs. Among those who

Although US authorities had no way of knowing it at the time, the Japanese had actually already given up on the balloon bomb mission in April. There were still thousands of bombs unaccounted for, though, so the danger persisted. And bombs are still being found. Two were discovered in recent years in British Columbia, Canada, one in 2014 and one in 2019.

heard the rumblings were people in the incarceration centers—including Yuzuru Takeshita and his siblings at Tule Lake. "I don't know where the rumor came from, it may be that the radio was broadcasting some incidents involving balloon bombs, but there was rumor throughout the camp that there were balloon bombs flying over the Pacific from Japan," Takeshita later recalled. "So we stood out . . . gazing up at the sky trying to locate, spot, one of these balloons. Two of my younger brothers, in jest, said, 'Hey, I see it, I see it,' and so everybody would gather around and say 'where, where, where,' and we never really saw it." They never did get any concrete information. He said, "We were left with the question: Was there really such a weapon used by the Japanese in that war?"

Takeshita would not know the answer to that question for forty years. But in a tiny town just a little more than an hour north of where he was searching the sky in vain, several families were finding out firsthand exactly what the Japanese had planned.

A news blackout of this nature would be impossible today.
Video clips would be posted on social media in a heartbeat!

CHAPTER EIGHT

Saturday morning, May 5, 1945. It was a perfect day for a picnic. The sun was shining in Bly, Oregon. Archie Mitchell was the new pastor in town, and he was taking some of the Sunday school students from his church on an outing. They were going to pack up lunches and go fishing. He and his wife, Elsie, were practically newlyweds, married less than two years. Pregnant with their first child, Elsie hadn't been feeling that well. She had baked a chocolate cake for the kids but had planned to stay behind. Then at the last minute she changed her mind and decided to join the fun.

The Mitchells headed toward one of the picturesque streams up on Gearhart Mountain, a little over ten miles from Bly. It was a good area for catching trout, and Archie was looking forward to getting to know some of his students better. Sherman Shoemaker, Edward Engen, Jay Gifford, and siblings Dick and Joan Patzke were all in tow. Joan's best friend, Annie Fagan, had been hoping to join them as well, but her parents ending up changing plans.

(Above) The Mitchell Recreation Area

Clockwise from top left: Sherman Shoemaker, Edward Engen, Elise and Archie Mitchell, Dick Patzke

91

Not far from their destination, the rowdy group passed one of their other classmates, Elaine Richardson, who was busy helping her parents herd some steers. "I was sitting on my horse and here comes this old, old car with the kids hanging out the windows hollering at me," she later said. "They wanted me to go, and I wanted to go with them." Elaine's dad needed her, though, and told her no. Not long after they drove off, she heard an explosion.

"This big boom just rattled the ground," she remembered. "Shook the ground under my feet." Within minutes, a Forest Service truck pulled up where she was and the driver told her, "Don't you move. You stay there."

She did move, though. The noise seemed to have come from the direction Archie Mitchell had traveled up Dairy Creek Road, so Elaine and her parents set off to see what had caused the noise. It didn't take them long to find out.

"LOOK WHAT I FOUND, DEAR!"

Road conditions had been affected by runoff from melting mountain snow, making the road muddy and riddled with potholes. Richard "Jumbo" Barnhouse, a Forest Service worker, was repairing the road with two other men when the Mitchells came along, and they advised the group that it would be difficult to drive any farther up the mountain. Nearby Salt Spring seemed as good a place as any to stop for their picnic, so Archie found a place to pull over and park the car.

While he was unloading the gear, the kids ran ahead to explore. Elsie followed on their heels, perhaps wanting to keep her charges in sight. Something interesting caught their eye. Later that day, Barnhouse remembered that from where he sat on his road grader, he saw Elsie and the kids standing in a semicircle looking at something. The group was only about three hundred feet from Archie. Elsie yelled out, "Look what I found, dear!" repeating it twice. He hollered back, "Just a minute and I'll come and look at it," but it was too late. One of the kids must have poked or prodded whatever it was—and there was a massive explosion. The time was 10:20 a.m.

It all happened so fast. Four of them were instantly killed. The fifth, Joan Patzke, died just minutes later, as did Elsie Mitchell, but not before Archie, rushing to her side, had frantically tried to put out the flames on her clothes with his bare hands. Barnhouse was right on Archie's heels.

Joan Patzke with her mother, Myrtle

The Patzke family had already suffered the loss of another child less than a month earlier, on April 8, 1945, when their son Jack was killed overseas. He was a radioman, serving with the 347th Bomb Squadron in the US Army Air Corps.

The explosion had carved out a crater several feet wide and about a foot deep. Debris was everywhere. It was a gruesome scene. The other crew members—George Donathan and John Peterson—were close behind. The Richardsons likely arrived soon after that. All had to proceed with extreme caution, as they had no idea if anything else left at the site could cause further explosions. They had to leave the victims where they were until military assistance could arrive. Elaine Richardson later recalled seeing Archie, standing still. "He was in shock. I was crying. . . . I remember leading my horse up the road. I helped my dad drive all the steers up the side of the road, away from the accident."

Something else made an impression on her, too. "I was told not to look over there, but you couldn't help but notice that big white balloon—it was huge," she later remembered. In fact, this may have been what attracted the kids' attention in the first place. One of the accident statements from that day documented that "the balloon bag was stretched out at full length over some low bushes with two of the shroud lines hanging from a stump about 10 feet in height. . . . The balloon was complete and very little damaged."

"NOTHING COULD BE DONE"

Within ten minutes of the explosion, Barnhouse and Donathan had rushed back to Bly to get help and report the accident—first to the sheriff's office, then to the chief forest ranger, F. H. "Spike" Armstrong, at the Bly Ranger Station. Armstrong quickly phoned in the accident to the Lakeview Forest Office, then he and Assistant Ranger Jack Smith grabbed first-aid equipment and sheets and followed Barnhouse back to the scene. They arrived at about noon.

While Barnhouse and Donathan had been gone, Mitchell and Peterson had cut some pine boughs to cover some of the bodies. Ranger Smith later recalled, "Nothing could be done. . . . This was enemy action. The Navy people needed to inspect and make sure there were no radiological, biological, or chemical contaminants before anything could be handled or moved." Smith stayed with the victims.

By 5:30 p.m., various alerted military intelligence officers, a few army personnel, and some navy personnel from the Lakeview Naval Base had arrived at the site. As Ross Coen vividly describes in his book *Fu-Go: The Curious History of Japan's Balloon Bomb Attack on America*: "Immediately adjacent to the smoking crater was a tangle of rope and wires connecting a boxlike frame atop a twisted metal ring roughly the size and shape of a bicycle wheel rim." Four cylinders (more incendiary devices) and a bunch of sacks (likely the sandbags) were nearby as well. The investigation of the explosion site found pieces of the bomb and its device scattered within ninety feet of the crater. Smaller, lighter-weight shards were strewn up to four hundred feet away. Bits of metal had been blown with such force they were driven deep into tree trunks. By the mildew on some parts of the balloon, and a snowdrift found underneath another part, it was estimated the balloon had been downed for at least a month.

Although it must have been excruciating to leave the victims' bodies where they were all afternoon, it was a good thing they had, as two remaining bombs on the ground were found to still be active. Once a naval officer defused the bombs and removed them from the site, the bodies were loaded for transport. The balloon and the debris were collected from the site and taken to the Lakeview Air Base.

By 8:00 p.m., Chief Armstrong had left for Bly to talk with the parents of the deceased. These people were no strangers to him. Three of the boys were in his 4-H group, and some of the parents were good friends.

This must have made his job even more painful. Armstrong also needed to know what he was allowed to tell the press. That question would prove to have a complicated answer—an answer that would create further heartbreak for all the families involved with the victims of the explosion.

"I CAN'T TALK ABOUT IT. I CAN'T TALK ABOUT IT."

News had traveled fast that something horrible had happened up on the mountain, but there was a serious lack of information about what exactly had occurred. Of course, the families of the children who had gone on the outing were desperately trying to find answers. But no one was talking. And the silence was intentional.

The War Department had a major dilemma on its hands. Since the first sighting of these Japanese balloons, it had been struggling to straddle the line between maintaining secrecy so the Japanese didn't find out that their balloon bomb project was having some success and alerting the public in order to keep people safe from danger. Now the worst had happened: people were dead—*children* were dead—and there still wasn't a definitive plan on how to handle it.

One of the people put in the worst positions that day was sixteen-year-old Cora Mae Jenkins. Her parents ran the local AT&T telephone office, which served about a hundred phone lines for the area. Saturday mornings tended to be busy on the switchboard, and Cora was working as the telephone operator that day. That's why she hadn't gone on the picnic with her friends Joan and Dick Patzke.

One of the Forest Service rangers came into the shop. "He was white as a sheet," she remembered. The man put a call in to the nearby military

Cora Mae Jenkins

base in Lakeview saying that there was an explosion and that people were hurt. Cora recounted the instructions he told her: "I couldn't talk to anybody. Nobody could come in. I couldn't get out." He put her on the phone with the military personnel he had been talking to, and they repeated those instructions. "Talk to nobody; put no calls through."

But people wanted answers. They wanted information. They needed to know what terrible tragedy had transpired in the woods. Cora had no choice but to refuse to answer their questions and to deny their requests to put phone calls through. "They were yelling and screaming and waving their fists," she said. "Everyone was angry. . . . They knew something had happened to the kids."

It took several hours for some of the parents of the children who were killed to be notified. In fact, when Armstrong had driven to Bly to find them at eight o'clock that evening, he had difficulty doing so. Neither the Giffords, the Engens, or the Shoemakers were at home, as they were,

Diane Shoemaker

understandably, racing around trying to find answers. With rumors circulating and no solid information forthcoming, Diane Shoemaker later recalled, "the more the day progressed, the more alarmed they became. . . . Finally in the evening . . . one of the authority figures told my parents. . . . My father was asked to come and identify the bodies. . . . He was so shook up that he could hardly remain coherent."

Diane was in shock. Less than two years apart, thirteen-year-old Diane and her little brother, Sherman, were extremely close, "more like twins. . . . I was always with my little brother," she later said. "He could see the funny side of anything and he was a little comedian. . . . He made us all laugh." Diane was, in fact, yet another teenager who would have been on the group's outing, but she had chosen to go to Klamath Falls to visit a friend instead.

When Cora was finally able to leave the AT&T office that day, she recalled "crying and crying—Mom putting her arms around me, giving me aspirin. I went to bed. I remember saying, 'I can't talk about it. I can't talk about it.'" People were grieving. Her friends were among those who died; Cora was grieving herself, but she was forbidden to discuss the incident with anyone.

The small community of Bly was rocked to its core. Six of their members were gone. Long after the funeral, many remained devastated. Cora later recalled, "I was in a daze for several weeks," and "it froze right in my heart."

Elaine Richardson recalled the terrible toll the order of silence took. "We were sworn to secrecy so I could not talk about it," she said. "It was bad going back to school—all them empty desks. The whole town of Bly couldn't talk about it. Nobody said anything. Nobody knew I was up there. . . . When you're that age and they say you're sworn to secrecy you take it to heart."

"AN EXPLOSION FROM AN UNDETERMINED SOURCE"

The official cause of death listed on all six death certificates was documented as "an explosion from an undetermined source." The War Department wouldn't budge on its stance that the media should not be allowed to report on balloon bombs—even though the local *Herald and News* editor argued against the censorship. The brief news item that ran two days later in that paper, with the headline BLAST KILLS 6, ambiguously reported that the victims had been killed by "an explosion of an unannounced cause."

GERMANS SURRENDER

NAZIS GIVE UP UNCONDITIONALLY

Herald and News

In The Shasta-Cascade Wonderland

CE FIVE CENTS — KLAMATH FALLS, OREGON, MONDAY, MAY 7, 1945 — Number 10459

Official Announcements Of V-E Day Set For Tuesday

By ALTON L. BLAKESLEE
Associated Press War Editor

An Associated Press dispatch from Reims, France, by Ed Kennedy announced the signing of the surrender, ending history's bloodiest conflict after 2076 days.

The British ministry of information said Prime Minister Churchill would broadcast an official announcement tomorrow at 6 a. m. PWT, "in accordance with arrangements be-ween the three great powers," and King George would broadcast at noon PWT Tuesday "will be treated as Victory-in-Europe Day," it said, and Wednesday also will be regarded as a holiday.

A Stockholm dispatch said Germans would begin marching from Norway across the border to Sweden this afternoon, in accordance with surrender terms, but there was no information from Swedish officials.

The surrender to the western allies and Russia was made at Gen. Eisenhower's headquarters at Reims, France, by the German high command.

In Washington microphones were made ready for a broadcast by President Truman. Prime Minister Churchill, after a busy day at 10 Downing St., went to see King George VI.

News of the surrender came in an Associated Press dispatch from Reims, at 6:35 a. m. PWT, and immediately set the church bells tolling in Rome and elsewhere.

In the hour before the news from Reims, German broadcasts told the German people that Grand Admiral Karl Doenitz had ordered capitulation of all fighting forces, and called off U-boat warfare.

Joy at the news was tempered only by the realization that the war against Japan remains to be resolved, with many casualties still ahead.

The end of the European warfare, greatest, bloodiest and costliest war in human history – it has claimed at least 40,000,000 casualties on both sides in killed, wounded, and captured – came after five years, eight months and six days of strife that overspread the globe.

Hitler's arrogant armies invaded Poland on September 1, 1939, beginning the agony that convulsed the world for 2076 days.

Unconditional surrender of the beaten remnants of his legions first was announced by the Germans.

The historic news began breaking with a Danish broadcast that Norway had been surrendered unconditionally by its conquerors.

Then the new German foreign minister, Ludwig Schwerin von Krosigk, announced to the German people, shortly after 2 p. m. (5 a. m. PWT) that "after almost six years struggle we have succumbed."

Von Krosigk announced Grand Admiral Karl Doenitz had "ordered the unconditional surrender of all fighting German troops."

The world waited tensely. Then at 6:35 a. m. (PWT) came the Associated Press flash from Reims, France, telling of the signing at Gen. Eisenhower's headquarters of the unconditional surrender at 2:41 a. m. French time (5:41 p. m. PWT Sunday), Germany had given up to the western allies and to Russia.

London went wild at the news. Crowds jammed Piccadilly circus. Smiling throngs poured out of subways and lined the streets.

A sour note came from the German-controlled radio at Prague. A broadcast monitored by the Czechoslovak government offices in London said the German commander in Czechoslovakia did not recognize the surrender of Admiral Doenitz and would fight on until his forces "have secured free passage for German troops out of the country." But the Prague radio earlier announced the capitulation of Breslau, long besieged by Russian forces.

A BBC said telephone conversations were going on between London, Washington and Moscow in order to fix the exact hour of the V-E Day announcement by President Truman, Prime Minister Churchill and Premier Stalin.

Late in the day Prime Minister Churchill, emerging from his residence at No. 10 Downing street drove to Buckingham Palace.

It previously had been announced that King George VI would broadcast at 9 p. m., noon PWT, on the day the surrender is announced.

DECLARES SURRENDER

An announcement on the wavelength of the Flensburg, radio, which has been carrying German communiques and orders for several days, said:

"German men and women! The high command of the armed forces has today, at the order of Grand Admiral Doenitz, declared the unconditional surrender of all fighting German troops."

The announcement was attributed to the new German foreign minister, Count Schwerin von Krosigk.

Crowds gathered in the flag-decked streets of London and crowded about microphones. Prime Minister Churchill had arranged to go on the BBC with the official allied announcement whenever it was ready. It was announced last week that King George VI would broadcast to his empire at

(Continued on Page Six)

BLAST KILLS 6

The Day's News

By FRANK JENKINS

E news is rather badly crambled as these words written, but this seems to bout what happened:

e Germans finally got toer some kind of central ority (the names mentioned new to most of us). These h-hitters (a Colonel General and a General Admiral dburg) called off the war at eral Eisenhower's headquartt a little red schoolhouse at ns, in France, and apparent-IGNED THE PAPERS.

me time thereafter they got of a microphone and ind in considerable melo-atics over the air about the ted German people who fought heroically for nearx years and should be given ak now that they have been d and admit it.

• • •

KING the news on the fly, ot even waiting for the first ce, Edward Kennedy, an exnced and responsible AP ter, got his office in Lonon the phone, told what had ened and added: "That's al, get it OUT!"

e London office of the AP et it out, whishing it somethrough the censorship in xcitement, and so the news o this country and started e V-E Day wheels that had held in readiness so long.

• • •

ems to be true enough.

t there's a mix-up. Maybe body put something over on ussians (there is no account r that the Russians have d off the war; in fact, they to be still shooting.)

yway shortly before noon has been no joint OF-AL announcement from ington, London and Mos-and the celebrations that oing on as these words are n are unofficial and sponus (perhaps all the more ne for that reason.)

• • •

AP is in the doghouse.

NS says this morning it has ed the following dispatch supreme allied headquart-Paris: "Allied military rities ordered suspension Associated Press' filing of dispatches from every-in the European theater erations as a result of ICATION of a dispatch Germany had surrendered ditionally."

UP says it has received r word. (The UP got into ghouse in the wind-up of st war, and knows how it It is doubtless just human to get a certain amount

ontinued on Page Six)

FIVE CHILDREN, PASTOR'S WIFE IN EXPLOSION

Fishing Jaunt Proves Fatal To Bly Residents

Five children and a minister's wife, all residents of Bly, were killed instantly by an explosion of unannounced cause while on a fishing trip in the Gearhart mountain area just inside Lake county and about 65 miles from Klamath Falls.

One of the members of the party found an object, others went to investigate, and the blast followec.

Killed

The dead:

Mrs. Elsie Mitchell, wife of Rev. Archie Mitchell of Bly, who was the lone survivor of the incident.

Jay Gifford, 12, son of Mr. and Mrs. N. L. Gifford.

Eddie Engen, 13, son of Mr. and Mrs. Einar Engen.

Sherman Shoemaker, 12, son of Mr. and Mrs. J. L. Shoemaker.

Joan Patzke, 11, and **Dick Patzke,** 13, son and daughter of Mr. and Mrs. Frank Patzke.

Rev. and Mrs. Mitchell and the five youngsters went out on the fishing journey Saturday morning. They fished in a creek on the Bly-Dairy creek road.

Find Object

Rev. Mitchell drove the car f.r a distance while the others walked in the woods. When the object was sighted, they called to Rev. Mitchell. He left the car, approached the group, and was about 40 feet away when the explosion occurred.

All but Mrs. Mitchell were

(Continued on Page Six)

Norman Dwight Reported Safe

Sgt. Norman E. Dwight, U. S. army air corps, son of Rev. and Mrs. A. L. Dwight, 823 Walnut, has been reported safe, according to an unofficial message. He was reported missing in action over Germany on February 13, 1945.

According to the message received by his parents, Dwight was a prisoner of war and has been liberated by an allied drive. He entered the service in June, 1943, and was sent overseas in October of 1944. He was an engineer and gunner on a B-26.

Page 1, November 11, 1918

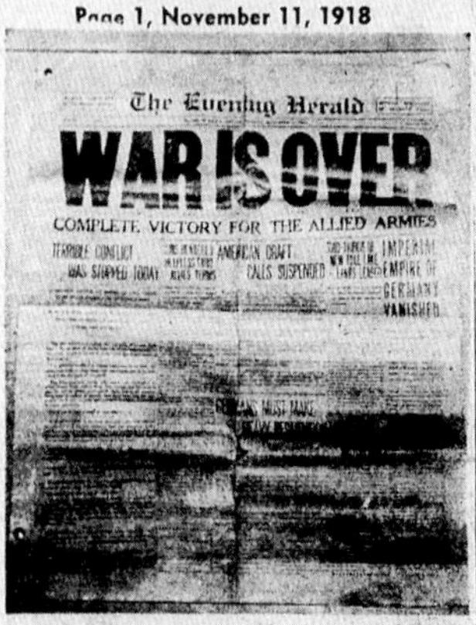
The Evening Herald

WAR IS OVER

COMPLETE VICTORY FOR THE ALLIED ARMIES

TERRIBLE CONFLICT WAS STOPPED TODAY

AMERICAN DRAFT CALLS SUSPENDED

IMPERIAL EMPIRE OF GERMANY VANISHED

Picture of the first page of the Evening Herald, November 11, 1918, announcing the armistice. German capitulation, on that occasion, meant the end of the World war. This time, Japan, Germany's ally in World War II, fights on. The Japs were on the Allies side in the First World war.

Klamath Greets News Of Surrender Quietly; Work Carries On To Beat Nips

Klamath Falls celebrated with sobriety today—the day of the surrender.

Aware of the intensity of Pacific fighting, there appeared no evid nce of the hysterical gaiety which swept the countryside in November, 1918, when victory of the allies over Germany was announced.

Stores, schools and business institutions were closed throughout Monday. Banks and theatres remained open.

Carry on Work

Military installations in this area carried on, well aware of their obligation to the fighting men in the Pacific.

Col. George O. Van Orden of the Marine Barracks, Comdr. R. R. Darron, Klamath naval air station, and Major John Hazlett, Camp Tulelake, commanding officers of these three marine, navy and army installations, reported no change in the daily routine and the granting of no additional liberty privileges.

"Work, Worship"

Col. Van Orden said the theme of naval shore establishments for the day is "work and worship" and that short appropriate ceremonies were directed with the realization that war with Japan still remains. Participation in community ceremonies was authorized but this did not include parades and the celebration was to be consistent with a period of mourning for the late President Franklin D. Roosevelt.

Navy suppliers, contractors and labor organizations early in the day were requested to stay on the job. No overall substantial cancellation of navy contracts comparable to army cancellations which may develop are anticipated.

Directive

Following is Col. Van Orden's directive to his men:

"In accordance with the instructions of the secretary of the navy, there will be no change

(Continued on Page Six)

Mixed Feelings Greet Surrender

By The Associated Press

America greeted announcement of Germany's unconditional surrender with a mixture of emotions.

Hilarious gayety, solemn prayer in the streets, a partial stoppage of business and an electric feeling of excitement swept from coast to coast.

New York's reaction was a snowstorm of waste paper that cascaded from buildings as people shouted and sang in the streets. Others openly wept and prayed on sidewalks.

Field Marshal's Body Discovered

WITH THE BRITISH SECOND ARMY, May 7 (AP)—The bullet-riddled body of German Field Marshal Fedor von Bock was discovered by British troops yesterday near a roadside north of Hamburg, where he apparently was slain in an allied strafing raid.

The ex-commander of the central army group in the German invasion of Russia in June, 1941, had been dead for about a week.

First Forest Fire Reported

The weekend witnessed the first forest fire of the season on land belonging to the Weyerhaeuser Timber company near Camp 4, and it was reported that the fire, resulting from lightning strikes, resulted in relatively little damage commercially. Although approximately 50 per cent of the reproductive stock was burned by the blaze, none of the virgin timber was destroyed.

By 5 o'clock Sunday morning, the Weyerhaeuser fire crew had placed a "trailer" around the blaze, thereby insuring against any further damage. It was reported today that the fire is entirely under control.

...re's Text of Surrender Broadcast to Nazi Nation

('s Note: Here is the text of o broadcast to German people ral Ludwig Schwerin Von Krorman foreign minister, announcmany's surrender. The broad-recorded by the British mininformation.)

man men and women! gh command of the armed has today at the order of Admiral Doenitz declared conditional surrender of ting German troops.

the leading minister of h government which the of the fleet (Doenitz) pointed for the winding ll military tasks I turn tragic moment of our to the German nation. r a heroic fight of alx years of incomparable s Germany has succumbhe overwhelming power nemies. To continue the war would only mean senseless bloodshed and a futile disintegration.

"A government which has a feeling of responsibility for the future of its nation was compelled to act on the collapse of all physical and material forces and to demand of the enemy the cessation of hostilities.

Noblest Task

"It was the noblest task of admiral of the fleet and of the government supporting him—after the terrible sacrifices which the war demanded—to save in the last phase of the war the lives of a maximum number of fellow countrymen.

"That the war was not ended immediately, simultaneously in the west and in the east, is to

(Continued on Page Six)

35 Jap Ships Downed; Nips Gain In China

By LEONARD MILLIMAN
Associated Press War Editor

American bombers reaching out from the Philippines and Okinawa, where Yank ground forces killed 23,221 Japanese in ten days, have sunk 35 more Nipponese ships and damaged 17 others, U. S. "On-to-Tokyo" commanders announced yesterday and today.

A Japanese breakthrough in central China to within 35 miles of the U. S. air base at Chihkiang was the only blight on allied ground offensives as Washington reports said 6,000,000 Americans would be thrown against Japan after V-E Day.

Progress Withheld

The U. S. tenth army resumed its general offensive on Okinawa after killing 3000 Japanese in last Friday's counterattack. But Yank progress was shrouded in official secrecy.

In the Philippines the 25th division captured the last hill mass controlling the Balete pass entrance to fertile Cagayan valley of northern Luzon in a four day battle. The 24th and 31st pushed northward on Mindanao still hunting for the main force of some 40,000 Japanese reported to be on the island.

Capture Drome

Australians captured the airdrome, two oil fields, major military objectives on Tarakan off the Borneo coast, in the newest Pacific offensive and in one of the oldest campaigns smashed to within three miles of Wewak on the north central New Guinea coast.

British forces captured two more towns in Burma as they began mopping up about 100,000 Nipponese stranded in the territory and harried disorganized units fleeing toward Thailand.

Chinese reported killing 3000 enemy soldiers in three continuing battles during which Chiang Kai-Shek's men shattered the left wing of the thrust toward Chihkiang. The breakthrough in the center was the closest Japanese approach to the threatened U. S. airdrome.

Troops to Increase

Victory in Europe promised to raise the American combat forces in the Pacific above 1,000,000 men for the first time.

Lt. Gen. Robert C. Richardson, commanding army forces in Pacific ocean areas, intimated the number would not be as large as the 6,000,000 mentioned by house military committee members, but said it would nevertheless be "a sizable force."

Interjecting a note of caution, Maj. Gen. Robert S. Beightler, commanding the 37th (Ohio National Guard) division in the Philippines, pointed out "we are only beginning to get into the tough Japanese fighting. Victory in the Pacific is apt to be a long distance in the future."

Join B-29s

Land-based bombers of fleet air wing two joined Superfortresses in carrying the war to Japan. They have been raking shipping lanes up to the gates of Tokyo. Last Saturday they sank two large oilers among a bag of 19 ships caught in the straits between Japan and Formosa—Japan's shortest shipping lane.

B-29s followed up today with another rain on Kyushu air bases of southern Japan—their 17th such strike since March 27. In last Saturday's three-pronged strike three Superforts were lost and eight to 15 Interceptors were shot down.

V-E Day Observed Here Monday

Klamath chamber of commerce announced today that the business district procedure for V-E Day had been carried out on Monday, and it will not be repeated in connection with any other developments relating to the European war.

Next victory celebration will mark the defeat of Japan.

AP Suspended From Filing News Dispatches

NEW YORK, May 7 (AP)—The International News Service said today it had received the following dispatch from supreme allied headquarters in Paris:

"Allied military authorities ordered suspension of The Associated Press' filing of news dispatches from everywhere in the European theater of operations as a result of publication of a dispatch saying Germany had surrendered unconditionally.

"This order was authorized fo. publication, but there was no textual announcement."

Similar word was received by The United Press.

Reds Keep Up Hunt for Remains

MOSCOW, May 7 (AP) — Russian troops, systematically examining the bodies found in the nazi chancellery in Berlin, have not yet reported finding Adolf Hitler or Joseph Goebbels, although the bodies of many members of the general staff, leading stormtroopers and high-ranking nazis—all suicides—have been found.

The Russians still believe that the report of Hitler's death was a nazi trick, and that the fuehrer is in hiding.

But there was still danger lurking in countless areas. People *did* need to be alerted. Within the next couple of weeks, the government decided that issuing some limited warnings about balloon bombs was a top priority. On May 23, the *Washington Post* shared the military's advice that "unexploded bombs may be found in isolated places and should be avoided." The piece further cautioned that "some may be buried in melting snow. . . . With the coming of warm weather and the end of the school session it is desirable that people and especially children, living west of the Mississippi River, be warned of this possible hazard." Still, citizens were directed to, as the *Post* piece reported, "refrain from spreading news of any specific balloon incident of which they may hear."

Within a month of the Bly blast, the government allowed reporters to identify what had caused those deaths. The *New York Times* ran an article with a crystal-clear title on June 1, 1945: SIX KILLED IN WEST BY A BALLOON BOMB. The text itself even addressed the media blackout directly: "The tragedy, the cause of which was kept a strict military secret until today, set off a wave of fear among southern Oregon loggers and campers who heard word-of-mouth rumors." The piece ended with a warning to "residents of western states to take precautions against the sporadic balloon-bomb attacks on the United States by unmanned balloons released from the enemy homeland." A similar piece by the *Washington Post* came out on the same day.

Meanwhile, other authorities, who had been sitting on information due to the media blackout, came forward. In August, Michigan state police disclosed that two separate Japanese balloon bombs had been found in May—one near Detroit and another near Grand Rapids. A third balloon was sighted while still aloft. A navy plane tried to shoot it down, but at

(Left) The news story that ran in the (Klamath Falls) Herald and News on May 7, 1945, did not identify balloon bombs as the cause of the explosion in Bly. This was the same day Germany surrendered, which is the headline dominating this newspaper as well as newspapers across the country.

seventeen thousand feet, the pilot was still too far below it and couldn't catch it before the balloon became obscured by clouds. That same month, the *Beatrice Daily Sun* reported that balloon bombs had been found in seven different areas of Nebraska.

"We knew we were at war," Diane Shoemaker later said, "but the thought of war coming right to our front door never entered any of our minds." Now it was a matter of public record that six Americans had been killed as direct casualties of World War II—on continental US soil—thousands of miles from the nearest battlegrounds.

Downed balloons, like this one in Burns, Oregon, continued to be discovered.

CHAPTER NINE

The war in Europe effectively came to an end when Germany surrendered on May 7, 1945. The war in the Pacific, though, raged on for three more months. That is, until the United States unleashed the most hellacious weapon ever invented—the atomic bomb—on Japan. While the Japanese bombing of Pearl Harbor had brought the United States into the war, the US bombing of Japan was about to finish it.

"A TREMENDOUS FLASH OF LIGHT"

On August 6, 1945, the United States dropped the first atomic bomb on Hiroshima, Japan. A survivor of this event described seeing "a tremendous flash of light cut across the sky," likening it to "a sheet of sun." Another recalled that "everything flashed whiter than any white she had ever seen."

That one bomb slaughtered more than eighty thousand people on impact, orphaning thousands of children and obliterating five square miles of the city in fire and rubble. Words fail to capture that kind of horror. There is simply no comparison between this catastrophic event and any other bombing in our planet's history.

In a radio address to the American public, President Truman said, "Sixteen hours ago an American airplane dropped one bomb on Hiroshima. . . . That bomb had more power than twenty thousand tons of TNT. . . . It is a harnessing of the basic power of the universe. The force from which the sun draws its power has been loosed against those who brought war to the Far East."

Despite the mass devastation, Japan did not surrender.

Three days later, the United States dropped a second atomic bomb, this time on Nagasaki. In an instant, this blast claimed another forty thousand Japanese lives. The radiation released from both bombs poisoned and killed tens of thousands more Japanese people in the coming months.

By August 15, 1945, Japan's emperor Hirohito had surrendered unconditionally, describing the cause as their enemy's "new and most cruel bomb."

• • •

As you have seen, war rains deep pain—physical, psychological, or both—down on everyone it touches. People handle this pain in many different ways. Some bury it inside themselves forever, never talking about their experiences or processing what happened to them. Others try to find ways to make some sense of the senseless and begin to discover how to recover. Still others are moved to go beyond their own suffering and create ways to help heal their fellow human beings.

These compassionate, kind people are often remarkable in their ability to see outside their own perspective, to put themselves in others' shoes, and, if needed, to embrace forgiveness. And with forgiveness, perhaps there can be peace.

What more profound opposite to war could there be than peace?

Nagasaki was not originally intended to be the second target. The city of Kokura—where most of Japan's munitions were made—was. Kokura also happened to be where a huge percentage of the balloon bombs were made. Because of poor visibility, the plane's course was changed to Nagasaki.

CHAPTER TEN

August 10, 1987, was a warm, clear day in Bly, Oregon. World War II had been over for forty-two years. Yuzuru Takeshita was now a grown man, a dedicated sociology professor at the University of Michigan, in Ann Arbor. He was known to have an open heart—and an open door for his students.

On that day, he stood in front of the Mitchell Monument up on Gearhart Mountain. At the intimate memorial event, Takeshita appeared a humble messenger delivering gestures of goodwill from Japanese women who had made balloon bombs more than forty years earlier to loved ones of the six who lost their lives in the explosion at that site. But this was no small event he had organized. What he had actually put in motion was something much grander in scope, something that would continue to evolve for years and years to come. He had inspired people to want to heal one another from a war that had made them adversaries, from an incident that had linked them across thousands of miles and many decades. That Takeshita could

(Above) Yuzuru Takeshita speaking at the 1987 memorial service in honor of the Bly victims

(Above) On August 20, 1950, a stone monument was dedicated to Elsie Mitchell, Sherman Shoemaker, Edward Engen, Jay Gifford, and Joan and Dick Patzke. Five hundred people attended the dedication to honor their memories. The governor of Oregon, Douglas McKay (not pictured here), spoke at the ceremony, referring to the victims' deaths as war casualties "just as surely as if they had been in uniform."

(Left) Elsie Mitchell's parents pay their respects at the monument during the 1950 dedication ceremony.

make himself that conduit for peace was remarkable, given what he, too, had endured. Or perhaps it was *because* of it. His own incarceration experiences, his love for both America and Japan—and his love for *people* in general—made him deeply sympathetic to all sides. His wisdom, compassion, and empathetic nature prompted the actions that had led to this day.

But how had it all come to pass?

How did Yuzuru Takeshita—a teenager incarcerated at Tule Lake, staring up at the sky wondering if balloon bombs even existed—end up bringing so many people together more than four decades later?

And how had any of the Japanese women involved in this event—who had lived through the horror of America dropping atomic bombs on their nation—come to care about six American lives lost?

"I WAS COMPELLED TO REACT TO WHAT WAS HAPPENING AND DO SOMETHING"

Some people call it coincidence. Others say there is no such thing—that everything is connected if you're paying attention. Still others might chalk up coincidences to "being in the right place at the right time." Whatever your personal opinion, two years before that August visit to Bly, various jigsaw puzzle pieces of Takeshita's life began to fit together.

As part of his work as a sociologist, Takeshita studied population planning and was consulted on several projects in Malaysia, Korea, Taiwan, and Japan. When he was traveling to Asia, he often took the opportunity to visit friends in Japan. During one of these trips in 1985, Takeshita stopped in the village where he had spent six years with his grandfather and visited his childhood friend Kazuyoshi Inoue. Inoue was married to a woman named Toshiko. During the course of their conversation, she mentioned

Yuzuru Takeshita with Kazuyoshi and Toshiko Inoue during a visit to Japan

that a TV program was being made about how Japanese schoolgirls were mobilized during the war to make paper balloons for the bomb project—and that she had been one of those schoolgirls.

Toshiko Inoue's story sent Takeshita's mind racing back to the day he and his brothers searched the sky outside their barracks at Tule Lake in hopes of catching a glimpse of one of the rumored balloons. Now, forty years later, he was learning that people he actually knew were involved and that the rumors had been true! Toshiko Inoue did not know whether the balloons had been effective or what the outcome of the project had been, but she had heard that there was information about it at the Smithsonian National Air and Space Museum in Washington, DC. Takeshita was amazed.

Once back in the States, he visited the Smithsonian to do some research. There, on the wall, was a description of the balloon bomb project and a map

In case you are wondering why Takeshita had never simply googled this information before the 1985 conversation with Toshiko Inoue and already known all about it—are you ready for this?—the internet did not yet exist!

showing where several hundred of the balloons had landed. The description also included information about the explosion that had occurred on Gearhart Mountain. He was stunned to discover how close he had been to the tragedy when it happened—just fifty miles from Tule Lake. As he read on, he came to the names and ages of the six people who had been killed. He stood there, looking at them, and could not help but think of his own daughter, Junko, who at that time was quite close in age to the children who had died. "I saw these names and it shook me," he later recalled.

"Immediately, I wrote back to my friend's wife with the list of names and their ages, and asked her and her classmates, when they talk about the balloon bomb, to offer prayer for them."

The following year, in 1986, Takeshita was invited to be a visiting professor in Japan, so he, his wife, Sun, and daughter, Junko, moved there temporarily. One morning, Takeshita happened to see a show on television that featured a former schoolteacher talking about the balloon bombs. The teacher's name was Yoshiko Hisaga. In discussing the history, Hisaga remarked that it was fortunate the balloons had killed only six people. But Takeshita found himself reacting strongly to the word *only*. It bothered him deeply. As it turned out, Hisaga had not been alone in her perspective.

"To tell you the truth, when I heard that six people had died," Toshiko Inoue later told filmmaker Ilana Sol, "it might seem a bit insensitive to say this, but the emotion I felt was that in war, people kill and are killed. With that notion of war, I did at first think that it was *only* six people who died."

A few months after Takeshita saw Hisaga on television, he attended a sociology conference in the city of Yamaguchi. At one of the talks, he noticed a woman sitting in front of him. He knew she looked familiar but could not quite place her, and it distracted him throughout the whole session. Finally, he realized why he recognized her. It was Yoshiko Hisaga!

Toshiko Inoue

When the talk ended, Takeshita introduced himself, telling her about his connection to the balloon bomb story and to Toshiko Inoue. They exchanged contact information. Still, he couldn't get the idea of that word *only* out of his head. Not long after, he wrote to Hisaga, sending her the names and ages of the six victims from Bly and asking her, just as he had done with Toshiko Inoue, to offer prayers for the deceased.

Hisaga responded by calling Takeshita and apologizing for using the word *only*. She told him she had shared what he told her with some of her former students, and it changed the way they had been seeing their own story. She told him, he recalled, they had "felt sorry for themselves for having worked so hard . . . in terms of the whole war effort that came to naught. . . . Suddenly with my message . . . their whole idea turned." As Toshiko Inoue later wrote, "In a war, knowingly or unknowingly, we are victimizers as well as victims." The women were moved to make amends.

The injustices of the world often feel far beyond our control. They may seem too big for one person to do anything about. But Takeshita knew that the choices we each make matter—that his simple gesture of reaching out to these women would matter. And it did. They invited him to travel back to Yamaguchi City, where he spent the day with Hisaga and three of her former students, listening to their stories. Although it is extremely unlikely that they were directly responsible for what happened in Bly, the knowledge of the specific lives lost there triggered for them, as Takeshita put it, "a transformation. I saw this with my own eyes."

"Once I learned the victims' names and ages," Tetsuko Tanaka said, "I started to feel a sense of guilt about what we had done. . . . We felt that if we folded a thousand cranes to deliver to the people of Bly we could express our deepest wishes for peace." The women asked Takeshita if he might get their messages to the family members of the Bly victims. In the message Tanaka sent to Bly in 1987, she wrote about the moment she learned the names and ages of the victims, saying, "Such a realization truly sent a chill down my spine."

Aiko Chisaka, another of Yoshiko Hisaga's former students from Yamaguchi, sent this message with Takeshita:

We participated in the building of weapons used to kill people without understanding much beyond the knowledge that America was our adversary in a war. To think that the weapon we made took your lives as you were out on a picnic! We were overwhelmed with deep sorrow and with the passage of time troubled by a sense of guilt.

Without yet a clear plan, Takeshita collected their messages, along with the one thousand cranes the women had folded. Years later, he reflected on how everything came together: "One thing led to another, and I suppose I was ready to pick up the ball, as it were. I could have ignored it . . . but somehow, I was compelled to react to what was happening and *do* something."

十
一

CHAPTER ELEVEN

Takeshita had learned the power of taking action from his own experiences, and from observing people who had made choices that had directly shaped his perspective of the world. He was acutely aware of how two specific people from his younger days had influenced him. One of them stretched all the way back to when Takeshita was a boy living with his grandfather in Japan.

"YOU TAUGHT ME RESPECT FOR LIFE!"

At that time, Japan was at war with China, and in December 1937, Japan marked a major victory by capturing China's capital city of Nanjing. Many of the Japanese soldiers who had fought there were from the region where Takeshita's grandfather lived. A village-wide celebration was held. Takeshita, alongside his neighbors, participated with pride.

Not long after, though, some of the Japanese soldiers returned from Nanjing. Private Morito Okazaki was one of them. Takeshita was glad to see him. Okazaki had trained with a truck battalion in the village before going to Nanjing. He was the youngest of four soldiers Takeshita's grandfather had given lodging to in their house, and Okazaki had taken the boy under his wing. When Okazaki returned from war, Takeshita went to visit him in the hospital. "He was showing me pictures of China," Takeshita later recalled, "and relating his brief experience there as a member of the invading army. He suddenly broke into tears and blurted out in anguish: 'We Japanese are doing terrible things in China!'" Takeshita did not understand what Okazaki was telling him at the time. At twelve years old he had, as he later put it, "the unquestioning faith we all had in the virtuous character of the 'brave Japanese soldiers.'"

But when the memory of Okazaki returned to him all these years later, Takeshita knew enough history to finally make sense of the soldier's cries. The Fall of Nanjing was one of the most brutal episodes in military history. Japanese soldiers swarmed through the captured city, killing thousands of civilians seemingly for sport, including women and children. Over the course of several weeks, the city remained under siege in a state of constant violence. It is estimated that more than two hundred thousand people were killed.

Takeshita thought back to when he was a boy, and how Okazaki had broken down in front of him at the hospital. He realized he felt grateful for the soldier's unguarded and remorseful reaction in that moment. "That I knew at least one Japanese soldier who was seriously upset about the behavior of his fellow soldiers in China back then," Takeshita later said, "served to help me regain my faith in the essential goodness of man."

With the memory of Okazaki very much with him, Takeshita tried to find him during a trip to Japan in 1986. He wanted to personally thank the man for the courage he displayed showing vulnerability and regret. He wanted to tell Okazaki how much of an impact he had made on his life. Although he learned Okazaki had passed away, he did locate his family and gave them a poem he wrote to express his gratitude. Takeshita's poem, written in the thirty-one-syllable form of Japanese poetry called tanka, read:

> *Your tears of remorse*
> *Shed some fifty years ago*
> *Kept my faith in man.*

> *To the schoolboy that I was*
> *You taught me respect for life!*

"I ASKED MARGARET GUNDERSON FOR 'AN AMERICAN' NAME"

The other person who had deeply inspired him was Margaret Gunderson, his teacher at Tule Lake. He remembered how she helped transform his thinking about doing the right thing and living responsibly.

Although the war had ended in August 1945, many detainees at Tule Lake had to wait for the US Justice Department to clear them due to their "disloyal" label. While the rest of Takeshita's family got their clearances in the fall of '45, he was forced to stay until March 1946. This may have been because he had briefly renounced his citizenship in an angry response to the "disloyal" label placed on him after the No-No situation. But the delay had resulted in what he grew to see as a silver lining—the opportunity to have been Margaret Gunderson's student and gain valuable life lessons that helped shape the man he became. Without his forced stay at Tule Lake, he would not have finished his education with Gunderson, graduating from Tri-State High School on December 21, 1945.

"On the last day of school," he remembered, "I asked Margaret Gunderson for 'an American' name as a way to mark 'my return to America.' She was delighted and came back a few days later with the name 'John,' which she said was the name of her late father, John Crosby, an immigrant from Ireland. I have proudly borne that name as my middle name since then. It represents to me the legacy I was privileged to inherit from her and a constant reminder of the importance of being a responsible citizen, willing to act according to one's convictions, as she did."

Around the same time Takeshita was reflecting on the roles Okazaki and Gunderson had played in his life, a business trip to Japan triggered a memory of yet another person. His childhood friend Tsugio Inoue had died during World War II as a kamikaze pilot. This was the friend he had been so close with during grade school in Japan—the friend with whom he had dreamed about life in the Japanese military together, before the Takeshita brothers were sent back to California. In hindsight, he realized that if it had not been for his family insisting he return to California before World War II broke out between Japan and America, there was a distinct

Even though the first of the ten detainment camps had closed in June 1944 and even though all restrictions against Japanese Americans had been lifted in September 1945, some detainees, like Takeshita, were kept until March 20, 1946, when the last remaining incarceration center — Tule Lake — finally closed.

possibility that he, too, would have grown up and fought for Japan, and he might have even lost his life in the process.

Takeshita felt grateful that his life had taken him on the journey it had: grateful to be putting all these pieces together, grateful to have a clear and developing sense of an opportunity presenting itself for peace that he could facilitate.

All of this was why, in the summer of 1987, Takeshita and his family made their way to Bly.

CHAPTER TWELVE

Most of the people you have met thus far had not yet interacted with one another—Tetsuko Tanaka and the other Japanese women who made paper balloons when they were girls, the beloved family and friends of the Bly victims, and the detained Japanese American teenager Yuzuru Takeshita. But they were about to.

In August 1987, Takeshita—joined by his wife, Sun, and ten-year-old daughter, Junko—were on their way home to Michigan from Japan. Junko had been put in charge of carrying the delicate cranes the whole way on the plane. They intended to make a stop in Oregon. When they arrived on the West Coast, Takeshita didn't yet have a concrete plan. He had researched where they were going, but he had only the last names of the victims' families to guide him. Bly was still a small town, though, even after forty years. The Oregon information operator had a phone number for

(Above) Yuzuru, Junko, and Sun Takeshita,
in 1987

Cora Conner admiring a string of cranes. The Mitchell Monument is visible in the background.

Edward Patzke—the older brother of Joan and Dick. Soon, Takeshita found himself talking on the phone with Patzke's wife, Ople. She invited them to visit and put Takeshita in touch with another Patzke sibling, Dottie McGinnis. Dottie lived in Klamath Falls, which was on their way to Bly. Cora Jenkins Conner—the young telephone operator at the time of the event in 1945 (now grown and married)—also got word of Takeshita's arrival, and she came to meet him. Within a couple of days, McGinnis, Conner, and the Takeshita family were on their way to Bly together.

"THE FAMILIES THEMSELVES FELT A HEAVY BURDEN LIFTED"

Takeshita had no idea what kind of response he was going to get from any of these people, and he was a bit nervous. Jay Gifford's father, Nyle, who was eighty-five in 1987, told a reporter, "I never felt angry. We were Christians, and we were forgiving." The friendly phone call with the Patzkes and the visit with McGinnis and Conner put Takeshita at ease. And while Edward Patzke did divulge to Takeshita that he had felt negatively toward the Japanese for starting the war and for his siblings dying in such a way, Patzke also assured

*Ed Patzke and Sun
Takeshita at the 1987
memorial event in Bly*

him that he didn't blame anyone for what happened. Takeshita later reflected that "the families themselves felt a heavy burden lifted."

Takeshita organized a small ceremony for August tenth. Draped over her arms, Junko carried the long string of one thousand paper cranes, signifying one thousand wishes for peace. Each colorful origami bird had been hand-folded by the Japanese women who, once upon a time, had been those schoolgirls hard at work making paper balloons to carry bombs— one of which had claimed the lives of the victims whose families gathered on Gearhart Mountain with the Takeshitas. "It was out in the forest; it was very beautiful," Junko later remembered. "It was just a very nice moment to be able to bring people together."

One year later to the day, President Ronald Reagan signed a bill into law that included a formal apology and $20,000 in reparations to surviving detainees. The law came into being after the Commission on Wartime Relocation and Internment of Civilians heard from more than 750 people and officially determined that the incarceration had occurred not because of military necessity but instead was due to "race prejudice, war hysteria and a failure of political leadership." On February 20, 2020, the state of California officially apologized for the discrimination, declaring February 19 "A Day of Remembrance."

Tetsuko Tanaka

Along with the cranes were messages sent by the women who came together for this effort: Yoshiko Hisaga, Tetsuko Tanaka, Aiko Chisaka, Ritsuko Kawano, Katsuko Maeda, Toshiko Mizobe, and Etsuko Shibata. They had all sent personal sentiments for Takeshita to share.

"We respectfully offer before you," Hisaga's message said, "a thousand paper cranes we folded as a token of our belated expression of penitence and with our whole-hearted prayer for your souls and for world peace. . . . We are feeling ever more strongly now the depth of our crime and seek most sincerely that you forgive us for what we fully realize is unforgiveable."

Tanaka's message said, "These one thousand cranes were folded one by one by some of us who made the balloon bombs, seeking forgiveness

120

The messages Takeshita read aloud in English that day were originally written in Japanese, which he translated.

In 1989, Tetsuko Tanaka sent a pair of beautiful lacquer Ouchi dolls, made in Yamaguchi, to Dottie McGinnis (sister of Dick and Joan Patzke). They were placed on permanent display at the Klamath County museum. Dottie McGinnis is shown, seated left, with museum curator Pat McMillan.

and with a prayer for peace and a vow that the error of the past shall never again be repeated." Toshiko Mizobe's letter included this powerful sentiment: "In a war we are all—victors and vanquished, young and old, men and women alike—both victims and directly or indirectly perpetrators upon others of pain and hardship."

Another message Takeshita shared, from Ritsuko Kawano, echoed that sentiment: "I vow that I shall join those who fight for peace by talking to as many persons as possible about the futility of war, and by insisting more than ever on the sanctity of human lives."

They did keep talking, including to one another. Takeshita, the women in Japan, the families in Bly—in different combinations, they remained in touch, writing letters back and forth.

"MY HEART STARTED POUNDING"

Several years later, after Takeshita was featured in a Japanese article about the 1987 event and his experience, there began to be talk among some of the Japanese women (the group of whom now included others who had been involved with the project during the war) about the possibility of attending the fiftieth anniversary of the Bly accident and meeting some of the family members in person for the first time. Takeshita agreed to help, plans were put in place, and a delegation of Japanese women traveled to Oregon.

On Saturday afternoon, May 6, 1995, more than four hundred people gathered at the Mitchell Monument. Takeshita read a poem he had written specifically for the occasion. Yoshiko Hisaga, the woman who had first asked Takeshita to deliver messages to Bly, had passed away three years earlier. She had told Takeshita she dreamed of cherry trees blossoming at the Mitchell Monument each spring, as a symbol of peace between the two nations. She wrote: "I'd like to make it a place where children can come to enjoy a picnic under the cherry trees and think about the importance of peace." In her honor, ten cherry trees were planted that day—six at the monument, and two each at the school and church in Bly. Kazuko Tanigawa—another Japanese woman who had made paper balloons during the war—had helped in this effort and sent along her message of peace as well.

Toshiko Inoue—the wife of Takeshita's childhood friend who had first confirmed the existence of the balloon bombs for him—had not initially been able to persuade her classmates to participate in these events. But she tried again after the 1995 gathering, asking Takeshita if he would speak with some of them about his experience when he next visited Japan. His meeting with nine of these women in September 1995 sparked a change of heart, and they asked him if he would help them reach out to the families. By Christmas of that year, a gift was sent of a traditional Japanese hagoita doll, dressed in a red kimono, along with a message of friendship from thirty-eight women of the Yame Girls' High School, Class of 1945. The following June, in 1996, sixteen people from Yame—including four who had sent the hagoita doll—as well as Tetsuko Tanaka, who had not been able to attend in 1995, arrived in Bly.

In the film *On Paper Wings*, Tanaka remembered how she felt that day: "As I was arriving in Bly, I saw Gearhart Mountain. My heart started pounding." Yaeko Yokomizo, who was also on the trip, spoke about it, too: "We were uneasy about what they would think of us when we stepped off the bus, but when we arrived, we were welcomed by a crowd of different people including a large man who gave me a hug. His welcome made me cry." Toshiko Inoue, writing of her experience, recalled, "I was tense, but

Yaeko Yokomizo

briefly, as warm, friendly eyes, with not a sense of anger or hatred, greeted us. The people of Bly were there to meet us as friends from afar. I felt, in the hands we extended to shake, a warmth between human beings with no national boundaries to block us."

"I LEARNED THAT HEART-TO-HEART COMMUNICATION IS POSSIBLE"

In actuality, the women had little to be nervous about. They were welcome guests. No one bore them ill will. Quite the contrary. "I just feel badly that they felt so responsible for this incident, because I don't believe they were," Elsie Mitchell's sister, Eva Fowler, said. "They were just little girls. . . . I think it probably was pretty hard for them."

Cora Conner felt similarly: "I couldn't feel any hatred for them any more than I could feel hatred for our boys that did what they did [in the war]. . . . I felt sympathy for those girls." She choked up as she recalled the event. "Our conversations had to be translated back and forth," she said. "But the feeling was there, the closeness, the lovingness, consoling . . . healing . . . it was there. It was pretty wonderful."

As a light rain began to fall, which several of the women later referred to as *namida ame*, or "tear rain," it felt particularly poignant to them. They knelt at the memorial with incense sticks lit in the Japanese tradition of atonement and said prayers, placing flowers and strings of paper cranes at the base. Afterward, people gathered at the church, shared a meal, held hands, and sang together. Reflecting on her experience soon after the trip, one of the women, Yoshiko Iwabe, expressed that it didn't matter that the people involved didn't speak the same language: "That night I learned that heart-to-heart communication is possible."

Left to right: Yoshiko Iwabe, Toshiko Inoue, Kinue Saito, Yaeko Yokomizo, Cora Conner, Emiko Kawahara, and Tetsuko Tanaka in Oregon, June 1996

Kazuyoshi Inoue, Takeshita's childhood friend married to Toshiko Inoue, who first told him about the balloon bombs, was also there. He wrote, "I would like to think that this trip is but a beginning of further efforts to seek peace and understanding among peoples." And Tetsuko Tanaka put the whole experience in context, saying, "I think both sides recognized the crimes of the others. America dropped atomic bombs on Japan and injured Japanese people, too. In a war, there will always be injuries on both sides. And when the words that we were forgiven were spoken it was a great relief for me personally."

She was not alone in this feeling. Conner's trauma from the terrible position she was in at the time had stayed with her. "They put a zipper on my mouth that day," she said, referring to the Forest Service ranger who

Left to right: Kinue Saito, Tetsuko Tanaka, Yoshiko Iwabe, Yaeko Yokomizo, and Toshiko Inoue at the Linkville Cemetery, in Klamath Falls, visiting the gravesite of Joan and Dick Patzke and Eddie Engen, June 24, 1996

told the young telephone operator she was not allowed to talk about the information she had learned about the explosion. "I couldn't talk to anyone, not even my mom." Even after the tragedy became public knowledge, she couldn't bring herself to speak about her own role in it. People in her community, longtime friends, knew she had been involved but weren't certain of the details. Nightmares haunted Conner. Her silence affected her relationships with friends for a long time after the incident.

It was Takeshita who finally offered Conner some solace from her silence. "It was a real relief talking to that man," she said. "I cried most of the time, but it felt good." Conner was dramatically impacted by the repair that was taking place. "I had been so traumatized by this thing," she continued. "It was all bottled up. And I wouldn't go up to the monument after it was put in place; I just couldn't do it. So, it has taken a long time, and John [Takeshita] was the one that really started the healing process of all this."

The effect on Takeshita was profound as well. In an interview a few years earlier, he had said, "Pearl Harbor not only sank the *Arizona*, but it really capsized our Bill of Rights." Now here he was, the only one at the event who had suffered incarceration during World War II. Some of the people there, who heard about his time at Tule Lake, approached him to say they were sorry. "They apologized for having supported that particular event," he said softly, "so there was a healing all around."

It had taken five decades.

Cora Mae Jenkins married Paul Norman Conner on May 5, 1946. She intentionally picked the month and day of the Bly bomb incident as her wedding date in order to add a happy, positive memory to the date.

十三

CHAPTER THIRTEEN

A Japanese origami folded paper crane has come to be known as an international symbol of peace. That wasn't always the case, though. The folding of paper cranes dates back to the sixteenth century, and in Japanese folklore cranes are revered and thought to live for one thousand years. Detailed instructions on how to fold a thousand paper cranes can even be traced to a book from the end of the eighteenth century. But how the origami crane evolved into a wish for peace is directly connected to World War II and, thus, to this story.

Sadako Sasaki was two years old when Hiroshima was bombed in 1945. Although she survived the blast, Sadako was later diagnosed with leukemia—caused by radiation exposure from the bomb. In sixth grade, she became so sick that she needed to be hospitalized. One day, the Red Cross Youth Club visited the hospital to deliver origami cranes to the sick children. When Sadako asked her father why, he told her the legend of the

(Above) The Children's Peace Monument, in Hiroshima, Japan, was erected in 1958.

cranes, and that a person who folds one crane for each of the one thousand years of its life will be granted their wish. Sadako set to work. She folded and folded and folded, hoping to reach her goal of folding one thousand origami cranes. Her wish—to be well again.

Sadako's hospital room was soon filled with colorful paper cranes. When she met her goal of one thousand, she made her wish. Sadly, she did not get well. After Sadako died, her classmates wanted to create a memorial to honor their friend and all the children who died from the atomic bombings. Their fundraising efforts reached far beyond their own circles, to more than three thousand schools in Japan. More donations poured in from nine other countries. The result is the stunning Children's Peace Monument, located within the Peace Memorial Park, in Hiroshima. Placed on top of the nearly thirty-foot-tall tower-like monument, a bronze girl with outstretched arms holds up a massive metal origami crane. Hanging from the domed center of the monument is a bell in the shape of a crane that is often rung in prayer, with the inscription SENBAZURU, meaning "one

Display cases at the Children's Peace Monument hold thousands of colorful paper cranes.

The inscribed stone tablet at the base of the Children's Peace Monument

thousand cranes." A stone tablet at the base of the monument has a chiseled message (in Japanese) that reads: *This is our cry. This is our prayer. For building peace in this world.*

A few steps away, in display cases, hang thousands of strings of cranes that people from around the world have brought in honor of peace. "Every time I see the monument," Sadako's brother Masahiro said, "I feel that Sadako taught us deep compassion, which can lead to peace. This is what Sadako left to us."

So what does this have to do with our story? Sadako Sasaki was *just* one girl. The Bly victims accounted for *just* six lives. "But a life is a life, precious in its own right," Takeshita told a group of fifth- and sixth-grade students near his home in Ann Arbor, Michigan, in 1989. "Whether it is six, as in Bly, or tens of thousands, as in Hiroshima. One, six, ten thousand, millions, it doesn't matter. It's a life," he said. Takeshita was visiting these students after one of their teachers working on a peace project with them reached out. The students were folding one thousand cranes for the Children's Peace Monument in Hiroshima, and Takeshita agreed to help the cranes reach their destination. He praised

With ten tons of cranes arriving at the memorial every year, that amount of paper needs to be managed! Strings of cranes are regularly taken down by city workers, unfolded, and used to make recycled paper goods. Every August, some are used to make paper lanterns for Toro Nagashi, a festival that honors the souls of the dead by setting thousands of glowing lanterns afloat at dusk.

the kids: "This is a small effort. But it is small efforts that add up to become big efforts."

A year earlier, in 1988, Takeshita had taken a different trip with another string of one thousand cranes he and his wife had folded with their daughter, Junko. Likely with Private Morito Okazaki on his mind, Takeshita's journey that year was to China, to the site of a monument dedicated to the lives lost during the Fall of Nanjing.

It was his own gesture of peace, a lifetime in the making.

Left to right: Student Chi Chi Ozor, graduate assistant Kanae Tanigawa, Yuzuru Takeshita, and student Elaine Stiehl admire a string of one hundred paper cranes made by students at the Ann Arbor Haisley Elementary School, in Michigan.

CHAPTER FOURTEEN

As you've seen, the interactions among the family members of the victims in Bly, the Japanese women, and Yuzuru Takeshita were intensely healing and gratifying. But there was still one person holding on to devastating feelings of shame and guilt from the past. This story began in 1945 with Diane Shoemaker, the young teen who, in a moment of rage over her brother's death, had imagined blowing up the Tule Lake Relocation Center in the name of revenge.

Even as a teen, Shoemaker knew deep down she would never have actually pursued her plan. In a phone conversation with me seventy years after the Bly explosion, she said, "The anger didn't linger long. It was something that was red hot at the beginning because I was in disbelief. . . . I was grief-stricken and felt helpless . . . but I became able to deal with those feelings and then felt ashamed that I had really transgressed."

It was certainly understandable that the shock of the event had been extremely hard to process. She recalled the details of the funeral to me as clearly as if it had just happened, her voice still cracking at the memory: "All those little caskets were up there, they were all sealed so no one could see inside. Those were my friends, those were my Sunday school friends. Everybody knew everybody, so you can imagine the calamity of the feelings I felt." Shoemaker's parents had also shielded her from witnessing the condition of her brother right after the accident. "My parents," she told filmmaker Ilana Sol in 2004, "did not feel it would be good for me to have a graphic description of this, so the only information I could get . . . was that my brother was dead and that I wouldn't ever be able to see him again. . . . I didn't believe it. . . . I thought they had made a horrible mistake. . . . I kept saying, 'Did you look, did they look everywhere?' . . . In my childish mind, I kept thinking they'd made a mistake." The news was too difficult for her to really grasp in those moments, back in May 1945. She had not been able to accept that her brother was gone.

"WHAT WILL HE THINK OF ME?"

When Takeshita visited Bly in 1987, Diane Shoemaker Jordan (by then, grown and married) experienced a jolt of realization that she had not yet come to terms with the shame she felt over her teenage thoughts of revenge, however fleeting they had been. "After I . . . discovered that he had been in that internment camp at Tule Lake and how he had suffered, then the guilt feelings I had were just really hard to live with." She was plagued by the thought that had she actually gone through with her idea, she might have killed the boy who had grown up to become this remarkable man. At first, she couldn't bear to admit this to him. "I thought, what will he think of me?"

It took her a couple of years to gather enough courage to share this with Takeshita. Even after he started writing her letters, she couldn't bring herself to write back. But eventually, she did, both apologizing for her own thoughts in May 1945 as well as offering a more general apology for the wartime incarceration. In the film *On Paper Wings*, she says about her letter, "I had begged their forgiveness, and asked them to remember that I was only a child when I felt that way."

His reply, not surprisingly, was loving and kind. "I do not blame you at all for having felt the way you did towards those of us who were at Tule Lake," he wrote her. "I have nothing but the deepest respect for your demonstration of love for your younger brother and concern for your parents who agonized over their loss. My family and I cried as we read your letter. Thank you, thank you, thank you, thank you for writing! I know it was not easy." He continued, sharing his thoughts and prayers for peace and the prevention of conflict. Before signing off, he added, "Diane, you didn't have to apologize for how you felt or for our internment, though it is very thoughtful of you to offer it. My bitterness, too, is long gone. Somehow fate has brought us close together. We cherish the warm friendship that has evolved from our experiences that strangely got intertwined without our being aware for such a long time."

More than twenty-five years after Takeshita sent this note to Diane Shoemaker Jordan, she shared it with

Diane Shoemaker Jordan, holding a string of origami peace cranes

me, writing: "After all these years, I find his letter even more moving than when I first read it. Once more I cried. Who could hold back the tears while reading what came from the heart of this beautiful man?"

Takeshita was a big believer in correspondence, evidenced by the frequent letters and postcards he sent to the people you have met in this book, updating all involved on one another's news, sharing milestones and stories from his travels, or recounting another new coincidence or encounter of how the balloon bomb incident continued to touch his life in unexpected ways.

In a 1990 letter he wrote to the families, Takeshita reflected with quiet modesty on what had transpired: "I am humbled by the . . . graciousness with which every member of the families of the Bly victims has reacted to the little things I have tried to do to heal the wounds of war on both sides of the Pacific that remained unhealed for so long."

He also mentioned a piece someone had written about some of those "little things" titled "Peace Is a Chain Reaction." Takeshita's letter—referencing a recent visit he had made to the Linkville Cemetery, where Eddie Engen, Dick Patzke, and Joan Patzke are buried together—continued, "As I bowed before the memorial . . . I prayed for a continuation of such a chain reaction."

From then on, "Peace is a chain reaction" was a phrase he would repeat in his letters to the families. His sentiment seems a fitting way to end this story.

Wrongs will continue to happen. Tragedies will occur. Be kind. Right wrongs when you are able. Reach out to those who suffer. Build community. Foster forgiveness. Make neighbors of those you do not yet know.

Peace is a chain reaction.

EPILOGUE

Yuzuru John Takeshita passed away in October 2016. Throughout his life, he wrote and spoke out against injustices in such articles as "Sowing Seeds of Peace" and "Japanese Internment a Stain on Our History." In his essay "Re-Americanization of a Kibei at Tule Lake," he wrote, "In the aftermath of 9/11, I have written in protest of the Patriot Act and admonished the public about their treatment of our neighbors who are of Arabic or Islamic background and not to repeat the mistake that we allowed to happen during WWII to those of us of Japanese descent."

Takeshita had a long and distinguished career in academics, and after retiring from the University of Michigan in 1997, he and his wife, Sun, taught math and reading to children in their community through the Kumon Educational Company. Kumon, a Japanese teaching method developed by Toru Kumon, became popular in the United States in the mid-1980s. "I could not have found a more meaningful way to live out my golden years," he wrote, "working day in and day out with children

(Above) Yuzuru Takeshita, in 1990, holding a scrapbook with artifacts from the detainment during World War II

Margaret Gunderson and Yuzuru Takeshita, June 1993

and their parents of diverse backgrounds—White, non-White, Christian, Jew, Muslim, Hindu, and Buddhist! It is exciting to be working with unity of purpose for the education of these children who represent the diversity that is America."

One of the remarkable things about this man was his lifelong dedication to connecting people and to nurturing those connections. He visited Bly again in 1990, bringing with him several copies of Reiko Okada's illustrated book *Ohkuno Island: Story of the Student Brigade*, which documents her experience working in the balloon factory at thirteen years old. Okada had reached out to Takeshita after reading about the 1987 event in Japanese news coverage, wanting to send her own apology to the families, as well as several copies of her book as gifts. The following year, Takeshita established a sister-school relationship between the Bly Elementary School and the village school in Yamaguchi Prefecture in Japan. Those two groups of children sent letters back and forth.

The Mitchell Monument still holds a place of honor and remembrance. In February 2003, it was added to the National Register of Historic Places. "Most of America doesn't know this exists," John Kaiser, an archaeologist attending the seventieth anniversary event, said in 2015. "We want it to be a monument to peace," added Dave Brillenz, the Bly District Ranger, who was also present that day. In fact, since the 1995 event, several rededication ceremonies have been held. In May 2020, on the seventy-fifth anniversary of the Bly explosion, two of the six cherry trees Takeshita had planted at the monument twenty-five years earlier as symbols of peace between the two nations were still standing strong.

(Right) Memorial services continue at the Mitchell Monument; this photo was taken at a dedication ceremony in May 2021.

WEYERHAEUSER COMPANY
EASTERN OREGON REGION

IN MEMORY OF

ELSIE MITCHELL	AGE 26
DICK PATZKE	AGE 14
JAY GIFFORD	AGE 13
EDWARD ENGEN	AGE 13
JOAN PATZKE	AGE 13
SHERMAN SHOEMAKER	AGE 11

WHO DIED HERE
MAY 5, 1945

BY
JAPANESE BOMB EXPLOSION

ONLY PLACE ON THE
AMERICAN CONTINENT
WHERE DEATH RESULTED
FROM ENEMY ACTION
DURING WW II

TRUTH AND TRANSPARENCY

Before you close this book, I want to share something extremely important with you about truth and transparency in telling true stories. Weaving together multiple pieces of information and points of view is what doing research is all about. And when you're dealing with people—and history is really just true stories about real people—it can get tricky. Traumatic events can make things even trickier. Consider the following:

A traumatic event happens, like the explosion in Bly. Various authority figures and reporters question the people involved—people who have just gone through a terrible tragedy. They are suffering, and each person is likely to react differently to the shock. They may remember things incorrectly or forget to include things. Their emotions may color the details of their account. Once time passes, their memories may get foggier—or clearer. All of these things—and more—legitimately happen, without fault.

So what's a researcher to do? The best they can. Put all the pieces of the puzzle together and see what makes the most logical sense. Which bits of information corroborate others or seem out of place? Which seem like they can't be accurate or feel exaggerated? It's an imprecise job that is impossible to get 100 percent right. That's history for you.

I've done my best to write about the Bly events as accurately as possible. This is where transparency comes in. What is transparency? For one thing, it's that I don't expect you to take my word for things without proof. So transparency includes listing all my sources at the end of this book, so you have the power to check up on me. Taking it a step further, I'm also going to share examples of information that was conflicting, so you can see some of the choices I made as a writer.

In some reports, Archie Mitchell was quoted as having called out to the group not to touch the balloon, saying he had information about the Japanese balloons. But eight months later, he took that back, stating he had no knowledge of balloon bombs at the time. Richard Barnhouse, the Forest Service worker on the scene, said Archie Mitchell was inside the car at the moment of the explosion, but Archie placed himself outside the car, unloading the gear. There are also differing reports on whether it was one of the children or Elsie who prodded the balloon, as well as whether or not Elsie called out to her husband, asking him to come look at what they had found. And perhaps this is a minor point, but many sources spell Elsie's name Elyse. I made a choice to go with Elsie, as that's how her name is spelled on the Mitchell Monument.

So, now you know what I know. Ultimately, it's my job to do the best I can to get it right. And it's your job to question authority, challenge meaning, and decide some things for yourself.

DEAR READER,

I came across some pieces of this story while writing my previous book *Courage Has No Color: The True Story of the Triple Nickles, America's First Black Paratroopers*. The complex story I have told here did not fit into a book focused on the first Black paratroopers in World War II, but the emotional impact of what I learned in this triangular story among the families of the victims of that bomb explosion in Oregon, Yuzuru John Takeshita, and the Japanese women grabbed hold of me and never let go. I wanted to explore that story, understand it more fully, and give it the space it needed.

Healing occurs in many ways, and storytelling is a crucial one. It is a way to share the overwhelming power of the human spirit and our ability to heal ourselves and one another. It is also a way to express understanding and either ask for, or offer, forgiveness. I hope that by sharing this story, I have contributed to these processes in some small way.

Without Yuzuru Takeshita, though, there would be no story. It was his compassion, his loving heart, and his dedication to peace that created it. And through this story, he left an indelible legacy.

There is always more to learn about any story. And of course, this is one tiny tip of one iceberg in an ocean full of icebergs when it comes to the history of racism and discrimination. Following this are my source notes and bibliography, so you can find out more information. I've also supplied a reading list of fiction and nonfiction books for you. I hope you are inspired to read some of them—and perhaps more importantly, I hope you are inspired to research and write a true story from your own family histories. Perhaps you will discover a family story to tell that will help make the world a more peaceful place.

—Tanya Lee Stone

SOURCE NOTES

CHAPTER TWO

p. 5: "a date which will live in infamy": Roosevelt.

p. 9: "The sky was just black . . . rumbling thunder": Rosen.

p. 9: "They issued us bullets . . . we were at war": Tsukiyama.

p. 12: "the unprovoked and dastardly attack . . . Japanese Empire" and "remember the character of the onslaught against us": Roosevelt.

pp. 12–13 : "The radio said, 'This is the real thing . . . 'This is a Jap'": Rosen.

p. 13: "There was suddenly the concern . . . same race as we are": Rosen.

p. 13: "a zone of danger": quoted in Goodwin, p. 296.

pp. 13–14: "They put such fear . . . were the enemy" and "The hostility was all around": quoted in Chiu.

p. 14: "We had the face of the enemy": Rosen.

p. 14: "We'd hear that the person . . . a terrible time": quoted in Goodwin, p. 296.

p. 14: "the great mass of our people . . . ceased to be Americans" and "When she starts bemoaning . . . from public life": quoted in Goodwin, p. 297.

pp. 14–15: "is relatively tall . . . delicately boned" and "betrays aboriginal . . . heavier beard": quoted in Goodwin, pp. 291–292.

p. 15: "prescribe military areas . . . such extent" and "from which any . . . Commander may impose": Executive Order 9066, February 19, 1942, National Archives, https://catalog.archives.gov/id/5730250.

pp. 18–20: "When the Japanese attacked . . . would have to move," "Japanese fisher-men . . . of our ships," "Japanese farmers . . . aircraft plants," "Neither the Army . . . people involved," and "The many loyal . . . war effort": *Japanese Relocation*.

p. 22: "Regarding Japanese Americans in the military . . . is a Jap'": Rosen.

p. 22: "There isn't such a thing . . . can't be done": Hirabayashi v. United States, 627 F. Supp. 1445 (W.D. Wash. 1986), https://law.justia.com/cases/federal/district-courts/FSupp/627/1445/1974210/.

pp. 22–23: "My father had a jewelry store . . . lost everything" and "We just had to leave . . . one suitcase": Rosen.

p. 23: "the quick disposal . . . evacuees": *Japanese Relocation*.

p. 23: "My brother and I . . . into my memory": Takei, "Why I Love a Country That Once Betrayed Me."

CHAPTER THREE

p. 27: "customary in those days . . . the 1920s through 1941": written correspondence with author, August 31, 2020.

pp. 28–29: "I began to detest school . . . stay at home," "I did not want to leave . . . send to us," "Once again my self-esteem . . . Japan in 1934," and "someone came running . . . Pearl Harbor?'": Yuzuru J. Takeshita, "Re-Americanization of a Kibei at Tule Lake."

pp. 29–30: "Suddenly, the whole school . . . very uncomfortable": Sol.

p. 30: "In class and on the playground . . . intimidated us": Yuzuru J. Takeshita, "Re-Americanization of a Kibei at Tule Lake."

p. 30: "I suppose she feared . . . a very scary time": Sol.

p. 30: "To this day, my voice breaks . . . internment experience" and "suggesting pro-Japan sentiments . . . in any subversive acts": Yuzuru J. Takeshita, "Executive Order 9066 and I."

p. 33: "Because we were a family of ten . . . horse manure to this day" and "There was no running water . . . were very shocked": quoted in Snapp.

p. 33: "I was not going to let the authorities . . . my dual heritage": Yuzuru J. Takeshita, "Executive Order 9066 and I."

p. 35: "humiliating experience" and "greeted with abusive catcalls and obscene gestures": Yuzuru J. Takeshita, "Re-Americanization of a Kibei at Tule Lake."

p. 38: "We knew we were confined . . . mostly softball": quoted in Snapp.

pp. 38–39: "being optimistic . . . suffered from our internment": Yuzuru J. Takeshita, "Re-Americanization of a Kibei at Tule Lake."

p. 39: "faith in our American . . . in adversity": Yuzuru J. Takeshita, "American Concentration Camp and I."

p. 43: "I didn't want that stigma . . . the US Army": Ben Takeshita.

p. 48: "In high school . . . we had in the system": Yuzuru J. Takeshita, "A Flame Lighted Behind Barbed Wire."

p. 48: "Americans are not perfect . . . destination already reached": quoted in Romaker.

p. 48: "in those darkest hours . . . as American citizens": Yuzuru J. Takeshita, "'Relocation' of Japanese in WWII Is Flaw of People, Not Constitution."

pp. 48–50: "Like any other American . . . pointed at us!": Yuzuru J. Takeshita, "Shame of Relocation Camps."

p. 50: "The top of the barbed-wire fences . . . keep outsiders out," "how touched he was . . . by one betrayed by it," and "These were indeed agonizing . . . over the years": Yuzuru J. Takeshita, "American Concentration Camp and I."

p. 50: "If you were my son . . . burst with joy": quoted in Fincher.

p. 50: "Thank goodness . . . had I not been one": Yuzuru J. Takeshita, "A Tribute and Appreciation to Our Non-Nikkei Friends, Unsung Heroes, Champions of Human Rights."

p. 51: "It was hard to get anything . . . was like there" and "It was probably because . . . people to be living": *History Detectives*, season 2, episode 2, "Internment Artwork," PBS, 2004, http://www.pbs.org/opb/historydetectives/investigation/internment-artwork/.

CHAPTER FOUR

p. 54: "hose-like band . . . serpentine fashion": quoted in Webber, *Retaliation*, p. 124.

pp. 55–56: "Infuriated that mainland . . . to bomb America": Coen, pp. 15–16.

p. 56: "Now things are different . . . and the home front": quoted in Webber, *Retaliation*, p. 9.

CHAPTER FIVE

pp. 58–59: "I carried charcoal . . . fighting a war": quoted in Cook and Cook, p. 188.

p. 59: "My education stressed . . . for our country": Sol.

p. 61: "Gazing at the rising moon . . . toxic gas": Okada, p. 12.

p. 63: "The girls would have to . . . after a day's work": White.

p. 63: "It was work . . . could ever imagine": Sol.

p. 64: "Eventually, we removed . . . poisoned by carbon monoxide" and "the war situation . . . serve the nation'": quoted in Cook and Cook, p. 189.

p. 64: "It fired our determination" and "Student Special Attack Force": Coen, p. 28.

p. 64: "Our Red Blood Burns": Coen, p. 29.

p. 64: "You must behave . . . warrior family": quoted in Cook and Cook, p. 188.

p. 65: "I was shocked . . . was deafening": quoted in Cook and Cook, p. 189.

p. 65: "At six o'clock . . . duty through the night" and "The floor was muddy . . . across the pasty floor": quoted in Cook and Cook, p. 190.

p. 65: "Here, a girl . . . balloon to explode immediately": White.

p. 69: "Banzai!": quoted in Coen, p. 31.

p. 71: "I can't recall ever eating lunch": quoted in Cook and Cook, p. 190.

p. 71: "When we returned to our dorm . . . the work we had to do," "My mother gave her sweet bean . . . salt from my tears," and "slept like corpses": quoted in Cook and Cook, p. 191.

CHAPTER SIX

p. 77: "That mechanism is not a weather apparatus": quoted in Coen, p. 64.

p. 78: "We found a bomb . . . disposing of the bombs": quoted in Ross.

p. 81: "After one hour . . . its operating altitude": White.

p. 86: "Blow plugs would fail . . . for these malfunctions": White.

p. 86: "Such are the facts . . . meet this menace" and "Any balloons approaching . . . appropriate authority": *Japanese Relocation*.

CHAPTER SEVEN

p. 87: "Lift Secrecy Veil on New Enemy Balloon" and "Everybody was mighty interested . . . town clammed up": "Lift Secrecy Veil on New Enemy Balloon."

p. 87: "What's the matter . . . Christmas present": quoted in Coen, p. 68.

p. 88: "Ten thousand people . . . on American soil": quoted in Coen, p. 83.

p. 88: "The balloon bomb attack . . . going to develop into": White.

p. 89: "I don't know where . . . we never really saw it": Sol.

p. 89: "We were left with . . . in that war?": Yuzuru J. Takeshita, "Re-Americanization of a Kibei at Tule Lake."

CHAPTER EIGHT

p. 92: "I was sitting on my horse . . . wanted to go with them," "This big boom . . . under my feet," and "Don't you move. You stay there": quoted in Juillerat, "Honoring the Mitchell Monument."

p. 93: "Look what I found, dear!" and "Just a minute and I'll come and look at it": quoted in Records of the US Forest Service.

p. 94: "He was in shock . . . from the accident" and "I was told not to look . . . it was huge": quoted in Juillerat, "Honoring the Mitchell Monument."

p. 94: "the balloon bag . . . very little damaged": Records of the US Forest Service.

p. 95: "Nothing could be done . . . handled or moved": Smith.

p. 95: "Immediately adjacent . . . bicycle wheel rim": Coen, p. 4.

pp. 96–97: "He was white as a sheet," "I couldn't talk to anybody. . . . I couldn't get out," and "Talk to nobody; put no calls through": quoted in Nobel.

p. 97: "They were yelling and . . . waving their fists": quoted in Juillerat, "Honoring the Mitchell Monument."

p. 97: "Everyone was angry. . . . happened to the kids": quoted in Nobel.

p. 98: "the more the day progressed . . . hardly remain coherent" and "more like twins. . . . He made us all laugh": Sol.

p. 99: "crying and crying . . . can't talk about it'" and "I was in a daze for several weeks": quoted in Nobel.

p. 99: "it froze right in my heart": Sol.

p. 99: "We were sworn to secrecy . . . take it to heart": quoted in Juillerat, "Honoring the Mitchell Monument."

p. 99: "an explosion from an undetermined source": quoted in Coen, p. 9.

p. 99: "Blast Kills 6" and "by an explosion of an unannounced cause": "Blast Kills 6."

p. 101: "unexploded bombs . . . should be avoided," "some may be buried . . . this possible hazard," and "refrain from spreading news . . . they may hear": "Attempts to Set Fires in Forests Disclosed."

p. 101: "Six Killed in West by a Balloon Bomb," "The tragedy . . . word-of-mouth rumors," and "residents of western states . . . the enemy homeland": "Six Killed in West by a Balloon Bomb."

p. 102: "We knew we were at war . . . any of our minds": Sol.

CHAPTER NINE

p. 103: "a tremendous flash . . . across the sky," "a sheet of sun," and "Everything flashed . . . had ever seen": quoted in Hersey.

p. 104: "Sixteen hours ago . . . to the Far East": Torricelli and Carroll, p. 147.

p. 104: "new and most cruel bomb": quoted in Allen and Polmar.

CHAPTER TEN

p. 106: "just as surely . . . in uniform": quoted in Juillerat, "Honoring the Mitchell Monument."

p. 109: "I saw these names and it shook me": quoted in Japenga.

p. 109: "Immediately, I wrote . . . offer prayer for them" and "To tell you the truth . . . was *only* six people who died": Sol.

p. 110: "felt sorry for themselves . . . whole idea turned": Sol.

p. 110: "In a war . . . as well as victims": "Reflections on the 'Balloon Bomb' American Tour."

p. 111: "a transformation. . . . my own eyes" and "Once I learned . . . wishes for peace": Sol.

p. 111: "Such a realization . . . down my spine": Tetsuko Tanaka.

p. 111: "We participated . . . sense of guilt": Chisaka.

p. 111: "One thing led to another . . . and *do* something": Sol.

CHAPTER ELEVEN

pp. 113–114: "He was showing me pictures . . . terrible things in China!,'" "the unquestioning faith . . . Japanese soldiers,'" "That I knew at least one . . . goodness of man," and "Your tears of remorse . . . respect for life!": Yuzuru J. Takeshita, "A Tribute and Appreciation to Our Non-Nikkei Friends, Unsung Heroes, Champions of Human Rights."

p. 115: "On the last day of school . . . convictions, as she did": Yuzuru J. Takeshita, "Re-Americanization of a Kibei at Tule Lake."

CHAPTER TWELVE

p. 118: "I never felt angry . . . we were forgiving": quoted in "Seven Japanese Apologize for WWII Balloon Bomb that Killed Six in Oregon."

p. 119: "the families themselves felt a heavy burden lifted" and "It was out in the forest . . . bring people together": Sol.

p. 119: "race prejudice, war hysteria and a failure of political leadership": Report of the Commission on Wartime Relocation and Internment of Civilians, p. 18.

p. 120: "We respectfully offer . . . is unforgiveable": Hisaga.

pp. 120–121: "These one thousand cranes . . . never again be repeated": Tetsuko Tanaka.

p. 121: "In a war we are all . . . pain and hardship": Mizobe.

p. 121: "I vow that I shall . . . of human lives": Kawano.

p. 122: "I'd like to make it . . . importance of peace": Yuzuru J. Takeshita to Diane Jordan, August 18, 1993.

p. 123: "As I was arriving . . . started pounding" and "We were uneasy . . . welcome made me cry": Sol.

p. 124: "I was tense . . . national boundaries to block us": "Reflections on the 'Balloon Bomb' American Tour, June 22–27, 1996."

p. 124: "I just feel badly . . . pretty hard for them" and "I couldn't feel any hatred . . . It was pretty wonderful": Sol.

p. 124: "That night I learned . . . is possible": "Reflections on the 'Balloon Bomb' American Tour, June 22–27, 1996."

p. 125: "I would like to think . . . understanding among peoples": "Reflections on the 'Balloon Bomb' American Tour, June 22–27, 1996."

p. 125: "I think both sides . . . relief for me personally": Sol.

pp. 125–126: "They put a zipper on my mouth . . . not even my mom" and "It was a real relief . . . it felt good": quoted in Nobel.

pp. 126–127: "I had been so traumatized . . . healing process of all this": Sol.

p. 127: "Pearl Harbor not only sank . . . our Bill of Rights": quoted in Pyen.

p. 127: "They apologized . . . healing all around": Sol.

CHAPTER THIRTEEN

p. 130: "Every time I see . . . Sadako left to us": "The Girl that Became Hiroshima's Icon for World Peace: Sadako Sasaki and the 1,000 Paper Cranes," DW News, August 5, 2020, YouTube video, 7:12, https://www.youtube.com/watch?v=FzIB4LkVtUE.

pp. 130–131: "But a life . . . in its own right," "Whether it is six . . . a life," and "This is a small . . . big efforts": quoted in Oppat.

CHAPTER FOURTEEN

pp. 132–133: "The anger didn't linger . . . really transgressed" and "All those little caskets . . . feelings I felt": telephone interview with author, January 16, 2016.

pp. 133–134: "My parents . . . thinking they'd made a mistake," "After I . . . hard to live with," "I thought . . . think of me?," and "I had begged . . . when I felt that way": Sol.

p. 134: "I do not blame you . . . it was not easy" and "Diane, you didn't have to . . . for such a long time": Yuzuru J. Takeshita to Diane Jordan, November 18, 1990.

p. 135: "After all these years . . . this beautiful man?": written correspondence with author, January 20, 2016.

p. 135: "I am humbled by . . . unhealed for so long" and "As I bowed . . . such a chain reaction": Yuzuru J. Takeshita, "To the Bereaved Families in Bly, Oregon."

EPILOGUE

pp. 136–137: "In the aftermath of 9/11 . . . of Japanese descent" and "I could not have found . . . diversity that is America": Yuzuru J. Takeshita, "Re-Americanization of a Kibei at Tule Lake."

p. 138: "Most of America doesn't know this exists" and "We want it to be a monument to peace": quoted in Juillerat, "70th Anniversary of Bly Bombing Recalled."

BIBLIOGRAPHY

BOOKS

Coen, Ross. *Fu-Go: The Curious History of Japan's Balloon Bomb Attack on America.* Lincoln: University of Nebraska Press, 2014.

Cook, Haruko Taya, and Theodore F. Cook. *Japan at War: An Oral History.* New York: New Press, 1992.

Goodwin, Doris Kearns. *No Ordinary Time: Franklin and Eleanor Roosevelt: The Home Front in World War II.* New York: Simon & Schuster, 1994.

Mikesh, Robert C. *Japan's World War II Balloon Bomb Attacks on North America.* Washington, DC: National Air and Space Museum, Smithsonian Institution Press, 1973.

Okada, Reiko. *Ohkuno Island: Story of the Student Brigade.* Translated by Jean Inglis. 1989.

Torricelli, Robert, and Andrew Carroll, eds. *In Our Own Words: Extraordinary Speeches of the American Century.* New York: Washington Square Press, 2000.

Tuttle, William M., Jr. *"Daddy's Gone to War": The Second World War in the Lives of America's Children.* Oxford: Oxford University Press, 1993.

Webber, Bert. *Retaliation: Japanese Attacks and Allied Countermeasures on the Pacific Coast in World War II.* Corvallis: Oregon State University Press, 1975.

———. *Silent Siege: Japanese Attacks on North America in World War II.* Medford, OR: Webb Research Group, 1992.

ARTICLES

Allen, Thomas B., and Norman Polmar. "The Radio Broadcast That Ended World War II." *The Atlantic,* August 7, 2015. https://www.theatlantic.com/international /archive/2015/08/emperor-hirohito-surrender-japan-hiroshima/400328/.

"Attempts to Set Fires in Forests Disclosed." *Washington Post,* May 23, 1945.

"Balloon Bomb Explosion Kills 6 in Oregon." *Washington Post,* June 1, 1945.

Beser, Ari. "How Paper Cranes Became a Symbol of Healing in Japan." *National Geographic,* August 28, 2015.

"Blast Kills 6: Five Children, Pastor's Wife in Explosion: Fishing Jaunt Proves Fatal to Bly Residents." *Herald and News* (Klamath Falls, OR), May 7, 1945.

Campbell, Brett. "On Paper Wings—2008." *Oregon Humanities Magazine*, December 23, 2019.

Chiu, Lisa. "Oberlin Vouches for Them . . ." *Oberlin Alumni Magazine*, Fall 2013, 12–17.

Chordas, Peter. "60 Years after Sadako Sasaki's Death, the Story Behind Hiroshima's Paper Cranes Is Still Unfolding." *Japan Times*, August 1, 2018.

"Detroit Almost Hit." *Winnipeg Tribune*, August 16, 1945.

"Enemy Balloon Bomb Is Exploded in Canada." *Washington Post*, November 21, 1953.

"Faculty Profile: Yuzuru Takeshita, Personal Peace, Global Healing." *Center for Japanese Studies* (newsletter), Winter 2001, 5–7.

Fincher, Jack. "On Wings of Forgiveness." *Reader's Digest*, March 1989, 85–90.

Flynn, Meagan. "For Japanese Americans, the Debate over What Counts as a 'Concentration Camp' Is Familiar." *Washington Post*, June 20, 2019.

Frail, T. A. "The Injustice of Japanese-American Internment Camps Resonates Strongly to This Day." *Smithsonian Magazine*, January 2017. https://www.smithsonianmag .com/history/injustice-japanese-americans-internment-camps-resonates-strongly -180961422/.

Freedman, Capt. S. Ambrose. "Balloon-Launching Sites Found!" *Pacific Stars and Stripes*, May 11, 1947.

Gordon, Linda. "Dorothea Lange's Censored Photographs of the Japanese American Internment." *Asia-Pacific Journal*, February 1, 2017. https://apjjf.org/2017/03 /Gordon.html.

"Great Balloon Mystery." *Washington Post*, May 27, 1945.

Hersey, John. "Hiroshima." *New Yorker*, August 24, 1946.

James, Thomas. "The Education of Japanese Americans at Tule Lake, 1942–1946." *Pacific Historical Review* 56, no. 1 (1987): 25–58.

"Jap Balloons Still Menace Canadians." *Washington Post*, September 6, 1945.

Japenga, Ann. "After 42 Years, Japanese Heal Forgotten Wound." *Los Angeles Times*, August 12, 1987.

"Japs Bombed NW Detroit." *Daily Monitor Leader*, August 16, 1945.

Juillerat, Lee. "Cora Conner, 87, Witness to History, Dies." *Herald and News* (Klamath Falls, OR), December 22, 2016.

———. "Honoring the Mitchell Monument." *The Military in the Land of the Lakes, Journal of the Shaw Historical Library* (Klamath Falls, OR) 28 (2016): 131–143.

———. "70th Anniversary of Bly Bombing Recalled." *Herald and News* (Klamath Falls, OR), May 6, 2015.

"Lift Secrecy Veil on New Enemy Balloon." *Daily Monitor Leader*, December 19, 1944.

Moeller, Katy. "Bly's Brush with War Recalled." *Herald and News* (Klamath Falls, OR), May 7, 1995.

Morris, Arval A. "Justice, War, and the Japanese-American Evacuation and Internment." *Washington Law Review* 59, no. 4 (November 1, 1984): 842–862.

Nagata, Donna K. "Coping and Resilience Across Generations: Japanese Americans and the World War II Internment." *Psychoanalytic Review* 85, no. 4 (1998): 587–613.

Nagata, Donna K., Jackie H. J. Kim, and Teresa U. Nguyen. "Processing Cultural Trauma: Intergenerational Effects of the Japanese American Incarceration." *Journal of Social Issues* 71, no. 2 (2015): 356–370.

Nagata, Donna K., and Yuzuru J. Takeshita. "Psychological Reactions to Redress: Diversity Among Japanese Americans Interned During World War II." *Cultural Diversity and Ethnic Minority Psychology* 8, no. 1 (2002): 41–59.

Niiya, Brian. "Common Myths of WWII Incarceration: 'More than Half Were Children.'" Densho.org, June 21, 2016. https://densho.org/common-myths-wwii-incarceration -half-children/.

———. "Pets in Camp: Dogs, Cats, Canaries, and 'Even a Badger.'" Densho.org, August 26, 2020. https://densho.org/pets-in-camp-dogs-cats-canaries-and-even-a-badger/.

Nobel, Mary. "After 45 Years, Klamath Woman Tries to Heal Wounds from WWII." *Herald and News* (Klamath Falls, OR), December 7, 1990.

Okazaki, Daisy. "In Hiroshima, Japan, a Teenager Finds an Unexpected Home." *Afar*, July 30, 2020. https://www.afar.com/magazine/what-its-like-to-travel-to -hiroshima-japan.

Onishi, Norimitsu. "At Internment Camp, Exploring Choices of the Past." *New York Times*, July 8, 2012.

Oppat, Susan. "Students Renew Dream for Peace." *Ann Arbor News*, May 23, 1989.

Pyen, Chong W. "Local Man Remembers Internment Camps." *Ann Arbor News*, December 8, 1991.

Rogers, J. David. "How Geologists Unraveled the Mystery of Japanese Vengeance Balloon Bombs in World War II." Eisenhower Professional Development Program, Mineral Area College, Park Hills, MO. http://web.mst.edu/~rogersda /forensic _geology/Japanese%20vengenance%20bombs%20new.htm.

Romaker, Robert L. "Dove of World Peace Comes in the Shape of Paper Cranes." *Ann Arbor News*, April 25, 1990.

Romano, Renee. "The Trauma of Internment." *Washington Post*, June 25, 2018.

Ross, Paul. "Remembering the Triple Nickle." *Wildland Firefighter Magazine*, June 2005.

"Seven Enemy Balloons Drop in Nebraska." *Beatrice (Nebraska) Daily Sun*, August 15, 1945.

"Seven Japanese Apologize for WWII Balloon Bomb That Killed Six in Oregon." *Washington Post*, November 14, 1987.

Shenkle, Kathryn. "Patriots under Fire: Japanese Americans in World War II." Center of Military History, United States Army.

"Six Killed in West by a Balloon Bomb." *New York Times*, June 1, 1945.

Smith, Jack. "Bly, Oregon Balloon Bombing." Pacific Northwest Forest Service Association, August 18, 2002.

Snapp, Martin. "Children of Topaz Return to the Prison They Once Called Home." *California Magazine*, Cal Alumni Association, UC Berkeley, August 1, 2017.

Spurr, Kyle. "On 75th Anniversary, Bly Remains Connected to Tragic WWII Event." *Bend (Oregon) Bulletin*, May 5, 2020.

Swanson, Ana. "The Dark Chapter of America's History a Trump Backer Just Called 'Precedent' for Registering Muslims." *Washington Post*, November 18, 2016.

Takei, George. "'At Least During the Internment . . .' Are Words I Never Thought I'd Utter." Foreignpolicy.com, June 19, 2018.

Takeshita, Yuzuru J. "Executive Order 9066 and I: A Reflection after 60 Years." *Monthly Independent News and Culture Around Ann Arbor*, April 2002.

———. "A Flame Lighted Behind Barbed Wire." *Fresno Bee*, November 22, 1984.

———. "Japanese Internment a Stain on Our History." *Ann Arbor News*, February 16, 1992.

———. "No 'Farewell to Manzanar.'" *Pacific Citizen*, September 23, 1977.

———. "'Relocation' of Japanese in WWII Is Flaw of People, Not Constitution." *Ann Arbor News*, September 16, 1987.

———. "Shame of Relocation Camps." *Ann Arbor News*, February 20, 1972.

———. "Sowing Seeds of Peace." *Ann Arbor News*, June 11, 1995.

———. "War Souvenir Symbol of Healing among Nations." *Ann Arbor News*, January 1, 1988.

Tanaka, Yuki. "Poison Gas: The Story Japan Would Like to Forget." *Bulletin of the Atomic Scientists*, October 1988, 10–19.

Wellerstein, Alex. "Nagasaki: The Last Bomb." *New Yorker*, August 7, 2015.

"World War II Jap Balloon Bomb Is Found in Far Northern Alaska." *Albuquerque Journal*, January 2, 1955.

Wu, Katherine J. "California to Apologize for Incarceration of Japanese Americans During WWII." Smithsonianmag.com, February 19, 2020.

LETTERS AND ARTIFACTS

Central Utah Relocation Center Guidebook. http://exhibits.usu.edu/exhibits/show/topazrelocationcenter/item/21805.

Chisaka, Aiko. "A Message." Translated by Yuzuru Takeshita. July 1987.

Hisaga, Yoshiko. "Words Offered in Prayer to the Six Victims of the Balloon Bombs." Translated by Yuzuru Takeshita. July 22, 1987.

Kawano, Ritsuko. "A Message." Translated by Yuzuru Takeshita. July 1987.

Mizobe, Toshiko. "A Message." Translated by Yuzuru Takeshita. July 10, 1987.

Records of the US Forest Service, Record Group 95, Region 6, Portland, Oregon, Historical Collection, ca. 1902–1985, National Archives and Records Administration, Seattle. Box 36 (5 documents): (1) Confidential summary, May 7, 1945, Fremont National Forest, Forest Supervisor; (2) Statement of Accident, May 7, 1945, Merle S. Lowden; (3) Memorandum from F. H. Armstrong, District Ranger, to Forest Supervisor, May 6, 1945; (4) Statement of Richard R. Barnhouse, May 5, 1945; (5) Letter from L. K. Mays, Forest Supervisor, to F. H. Armstrong et al., May 19, 1945.

"Reflections on the 'Balloon Bomb' American Tour, June 22–27, 1996." Excerpts of essays, translated by John Y. Takeshita, August 15, 1997.

Report of the Commission on Wartime Relocation and Internment of Civilians. https://www.archives.gov/research/japanese-americans/justice-denied.

Roosevelt, Franklin D. *Speech by Franklin D. Roosevelt, New York* (Transcript). 1941. Library of Congress.

Takeshita, Ben. Interview by Virginia Yamada, March 11, 2019 (ddr-densho-1000-467). Densho Visual History Collection.

Takeshita, Yuzuru J. "American Concentration Camp and I: A Personal Reflection." Martin Luther King Symposium, University of Michigan. January 12, 1988.

———. Annual reflection letters to friends. Courtesy of Diane Jordan.

——— to Diane Jordan, November 18, 1990. Courtesy of Diane Jordan.

——— to Diane Jordan, August 18, 1993. Courtesy of Diane Jordan.

———. "Re-Americanization of a Kibei at Tule Lake." From *Trials and Triumphs*, Tri-State High School, Classes of 1945, Tule Lake Segregation Center, Newell, California. Edited by Terry Ishihara and Ben Hara. 2004, 82–100.

———. "To the Bereaved Families in Bly, Oregon." June 1990.

———. "A Tribute and Appreciation to Our Non-Nikkei Friends, Unsung Heroes, Champions of Human Rights: Remembering Margaret C. Gunderson." March 7, 1998.

Tanaka, Tetsuko. "A Message." Translated by Yuzuru Takeshita. July 10, 1987.

Tanigawa, Kazuko, and Kozo Tanigawa. "To the People of Bly." Care of Yuzuru Takeshita. May 1995.

Tsukiyama, Ted. Oral History Interview. Accession Number: 1990.481.41/RG Number: RG-50.062.0041. United States Holocaust Memorial Museum Collection, acquired from the Hawaii Holocaust Project. Interview occurred December 21, 1987. https://collections.ushmm.org/search/catalog/irn511112.

War Relocation Authority. Central Utah Final Accountability Report [for the Topaz Relocation Center], October 1945. Microfilmed by the National Archives, October 17, 1994. The Takeshita family's listing appears on p. 181. http://exhibits.usu.edu/exhibits/show/topazrelocationcenter/item/21805.

VIDEOS

Aderer, Konrad, dir. *Resistance at Tule Lake*. First Run Features, 2018.

A Challenge to Democracy. War Relocation Authority film, January 31, 1944, presented by C-SPAN's American History TV, *Reel America*. https://www.c-span.org/video/?323977-1/1944-film-a-challenge-democracy.

Japanese Paper Balloon. United States Navy Training Film, Restricted. National Archives and Records Administration (NARA). Department of the Navy. Office of the Chief of Naval Operations. Naval Observatory.

Japanese Relocation. War Relocation Authority film, hosted and narrated by Milton Eisenhower, January 31, 1943, presented by C-SPAN's American History TV, *Reel America*. https://www.c-span.org/video/?323978-1/japanese-relocation.

Rosen, Steve, dir. *Beyond Barbed Wire*. Kit Parker Films, 2001.

Sol, Ilana, dir. *On Paper Wings*. Film Is Forever Productions, 2008.

Takei, George. "Why I Love a Country That Once Betrayed Me." TEDxKyoto, June 2014.

White, Michael, dir. *On a Wind and a Prayer: The True Story of the Japanese Balloon Bomb Attacks on North America during World War II*. Michael White Films, Distributed by PBS, 2005.

READING LIST

FICTION

Brown, Waka T. *While I Was Away*. New York: Quill Tree/HarperCollins, 2021.

Chee, Traci. *We Are Not Free*. New York: Houghton Mifflin, 2020.

Florence, Debbi Michiko. *Keep It Together, Keiko Carter*. New York: Scholastic, 2020.

Jean, Emiko. *Tokyo Ever After*. New York: Flatiron/Macmillan, 2021.

Kadohata, Cynthia. *A Place to Belong*. New York: Atheneum, 2019.

——. *The Thing about Luck*. New York: Atheneum, 2014.

——. *Weedflower*. New York: Atheneum, 2009.

Kuhn, Sarah. *I Love You So Mochi*. New York: Scholastic, 2019.

Larson, Kirby. *Dash*. New York: Scholastic, 2014.

Nagai, Mariko. *Dust of Eden*. Chicago: Whitman, 2014.

Sepahban, Lois. *Paper Wishes*. New York: Farrar, Straus & Giroux, 2016.

Sugiura, Misa. *This Time Will Be Different*. New York: HarperTeen, 2020.

NONFICTION

Dawson, Eric David. *Putting Peace First: Seven Commitments to Change the World*. New York: Viking, 2018.

DiCicco, Sue, and Masahiro Sasaki. *The Complete Story of Sadako Sasaki and the Thousand Cranes*. North Clarendon, VT: Tuttle, 2020.

Gordon, Linda. *Impounded: Dorothea Lange and the Censored Images of Japanese Internment*. New York: W. W. Norton, 2008.

Houston, Jeanne Wakatsuki. *Farewell to Manzanar*. New York: Houghton Mifflin, 2002.

Marrin, Albert. *Uprooted: The Japanese American Experience during World War II*. New York: Knopf, 2016.

Oppenheim, Joanne. *Dear Miss Breed: True Stories of the Japanese American Incarceration during World War II and the Librarian Who Made a Difference*. New York: Scholastic, 2006.

Reynolds, Jason, and Ibram X. Kendi. *Stamped: Racism, Antiracism, and You*. New York: Little, Brown, 2020.

Stelsen, Caren. *Sachiko: A Nagasaki Bomb Survivor's Story*. Minneapolis: Carolrhoda, 2016.

Takei, George, with Steven Scott and Justin Eisinger. *They Called Us Enemy*. Marietta, GA: Top Shelf Productions/IDW, 2019.

Tunnell, Michael O. *Desert Diary: Japanese American Kids Behind Barbed Wire*. Watertown, MA: Charlesbridge, 2020.

IMAGE CREDITS

INDEX

Page numbers in *italics* indicate images and/or captions.

Pages cited in roman type may also contain images and/or captions.

ACKNOWLEDGMENTS

As always, narrative nonfiction works are simply not possible without the good fortune of discovering collaborators and keepers of information who hold dear the importance of getting a story right, and who are willing to share their knowledge. There are many people to thank, in that light.

To Hilary Van Dusen, editor extraordinaire, who graciously gave me the time I needed to finish this manuscript and her exceptional guidance along the way. To Hannah Mahoney for being the most wonderful copyeditor in the world, whom I have been lucky enough to have edit all of my Candlewick books. To the entire team at Candlewick, especially designers Nancy Brennan and Rachel Wood. To Sarah Aronson for always keeping the faith. To Liza and Jake for putting up with me when my minimalist response of "I'm writing" had to suffice.

To Reiko Okada for granting permission to reproduce some of her gorgeous illustrations from her book *Ohkuno Island: Story of the Student Brigade*. To Ross Coen, author of *Fu-Go: The Curious History of Japan's Balloon Bomb Attack on America* for sharing copies of primary-source documents with me that I couldn't access due to the Seattle NARA office being closed because of COVID-19. To every family member or small-archive researcher connected to this story who helped track down the many obscure photographs needed for my visual storytelling (as well as for the memories they shared of those images), especially Alla Powers, Krissy Sonniksen, Robert Mikesh, Debbie Dawang, Merlin Shoemaker, and Tim Conner. To Ilana Sol for sharing enthusiasm, insights, and resources with me from her amazing documentary *On Paper Wings* and for facilitating my initial communication with Diane Shoemaker Jordan and Toshiko Inoue's family.

To Diane Shoemaker Jordan for entrusting me with her correspondence with Yuzuru Takeshita, having enlightening conversations with me, and generally being a tireless cheerleader. To Debbie Gonzales for her invaluable research assistance in Michigan gathering Yuzuru Takeshita's papers. To Brian Niiya, at Densho: The Japanese American Legacy Project, for his expert review of several chapters.

To Laura Takeshita for her welcoming support and for putting me in touch with her father's siblings Ben Takeshita and Michiko Mukai. To Ben Takeshita for striking up a fascinating correspondence with me and giving me a deeper sense of the Takeshita family history. To Michiko Mukai and Wesley Mukai for generously providing me with family photographs. To Junko and Sun Takeshita for granting me access to a wealth of Yuzuru Takeshita's letters, article clippings, and visual materials, and, most importantly, for allowing me to gain insights and understanding through studying these materials.